A LITTLE BIT OF LOVE

A Little Bit
of
LOVE

Father Brian D'Arcy

This Edition published November 2003
© Copyright Father Brian D'Arcy 1995 and 2003

ISBN 1 873223 71 4

Acknowledgement

The author and publishers are grateful to the *Sunday World* for permission to reprint these pieces. Sources of quotations are indicated in the text. In some cases it has not been possible to trace original sources: the authors of any such extracts should contact the publishers to ensure acknowledgement in future editions.

Typeset by City Print, Galway
Printed in Ireland by Leinster Leader Ltd.

Published by
Boa Vista
31 The Bailey
Galway
Ireland

Contents

Introduction

Nothing that is worth doing, can be achieved in our lifetime;
Therefore we must be saved by hope...
Nothing we do, however virtuous, can be accomplished alone;
Therefore we are saved by love.

Reinbold Niebuhr.

My last book was *A Little Bit Of Hope. Love* is the reason for this one.

We are saved by love — God's love, the love of family and friends and ultimately a healthy self-love.

Too often religion is full of duty. Spirituality is guided by love.

To love is to be vulnerable. As C.S. Lewis said after he found love late in life: "Love and your heart will certainly be wrung and possibly be broken. If you want to make sure of keeping it intact, you must give your heart to no one, not even to an animal.

"Wrap it carefully round with hobbies and little luxuries.

"Avoid all entanglements. Lock it up safe in the coffin of your selfishness.

"It will not be broken. It will become unbreakable, impenetrable, irredeemable.

"The only place outside Heaven where you can be perfectly safe from the dangers of Love is ... Hell."

I have this image of heaven that we'll find nothing new there. We'll wake from the long hours of sleep and nightmares and dreams and find that the arms which hold us will be the arms which have always held us.

We find love in the good and bad of life. We find it in the joy of laughter, the pain of brokenness, the wrenching of choosing paths we'd rather not travel.

We find it in the words of encouragement, as well as in the care of someone who points out how we might be better.

That is why there are sad and happy stories here. It's why I have used more short, sharp, pithy stories than usual. There are days when we can manage only a few lines.

As always, human stories are most powerful. From them, you'll find love in corners of your heart you thought had gone cold.

The best way to read the book is to pick it up now and again. It's not meant to be read at a sitting. Use it when the mood fits.

Much of what you read has appeared in a different way in *The Sunday World*. My thanks to them for their cooperation.

And no matter what else, I want you to find the strength to accept yourself as you are — to make your life an act of love; to see the good in yourself and in life; to be happy with growth, not expecting instant perfection. And, most of all, be an actor, not a re-actor.

Love liberates and empowers those we love to become their best selves.

Father Brian D'Arcy, C.P.   **The Graan**
                                                           Enniskillen

A Man of the Soil
At Heaven's Gate

I was reading recently a modern day parable. It's one which has been around for a few years.

Roughly, this is how I first heard it, many moons ago..

Once upon a time there was a lovely peasant farmer who lived and loved in Co. Fermanagh.

Like most people from the land he loved life and work. He enjoyed the feel of the soil. He got great pleasure from dirt on his hands. The best feeling in the world was the warm sun on the back of his neck as he toiled in the fields.

He loved his wife, though he rarely told her so. He showed his love for his children by being strict and fatherly and caring. His friends always knew that he loved them because he treated them as friends.

He talked to them, he laughed with them, he ate with them. He made love in the truest sense of the word — simply by sharing life.

He loved Ireland and his country. Everything about it was his. He was at home in Ireland. He was at home beside Lough Erne.

After many years he sensed one day that death was near. And as any man of the land will tell you, death itself didn't frighten him. But what scared him was the fact that he had to leave the familiar people and the familiar land he loved.

He didn't mind dying, provided he didn't have to leave home, his wife, his children, and his land, to do so.

But being a man of faith he was prepared to die. And to help him die he grasped a handful of soil as big as a shovelful. It was the soil of Fermanagh and he told his loved ones to make sure it was buried with him.

In due time he died and found that his loved ones had fulfilled his last wish. The soil was still in his hand when he arrived at Heaven's Gate.

But Heaven's Gate was firmly barred against him. St. Peter came to him and explained to him that he had lived a good life and that there was a place for him inside but that he could not spoil Heaven by bringing in a handful of Fermanagh's earth. He told him that if he wanted to enter Heaven he would have to drop the soil.

The man was reluctant to leave his soil. He argued: "This soil is the only thing I know. What's inside your gate I do not know. This soil is my life, my wife, my work, my family.

"It represents everything that has got me to Heaven's Gates, so why can't I take it with me?"

Peter was silent and defeated and left him outside the large locked gates of Heaven.

An hour later the gates opened a second time and this time a young child came out to him. She didn't try to reason with the man. She didn't coax him into letting go of the soil in his hands.

She simply took his hand and as she did, his hand opened and the soil of Fermanagh plumped on the ground. And with her tiny hand she led him through the gates of Heaven.

A shock awaited the man when he got to Heaven. Because there before him lay all of Fermanagh. Heaven was familiar ground.

That's the story and you can tell it about any place in the world.

But what does the parable mean?

It says something to me about the kind of God we believe in. Perhaps the most beautiful thing in the world about being human is that we love the things of earth. We love the flesh of the world. And that's a beautiful thing to do.

But perhaps the worst thing about being human is that we won't let go. We love our home here so much that we believe there is no other home.

True, there are some who are so heavenly-minded that they are of no earthy use.

And there are some of us who are so ingrained in the earth that we cannot recognise Heaven.

Perhaps that's what the parable means.

But perhaps it also means that saints are an unfriendly lot. And that unless we receive the Kingdom of Heaven as a little child does, we shall never enter into it.

Perhaps the innocence of a child who reaches out a hand of friendship rather than a list of dogmas is the more encouraging gateway to Heaven.

Ten Tips For
A Happier Marriage

Here's a sermon I'd love to give at marriages. But most people would think it too unromantic. And so it is.
Too practical a sermon at marriage could be inappropriate.
There is a time for talking straight and there's a time for romance.
If I were married myself, I'm not sure I'd be very good at these. But from the outside looking in, these tips could be a help.

1. Be courteous.

It never fails to amaze me how couples going out together can call each other loving romantic names. And after marriage husbands begin to talk to the wife as they used to talk to their own sister. Grouchily.
There was a time when men were supposed to be manly. Short answers and gruffness was a symbol of authority. That's outdated. If you're nice to strangers, be nice to those you live with. There's nothing worse than to hear a man speaking grouchily to his wife, or a wife making a laugh of her husband, or running him down in front of others. It's horrible.
Feminism has taken away many opportunities for courtesy. It's not fitting, in some people's minds, to open a door or stand back or let a lady go first. Whatever about your behaviour in the office, couples who are courteous and civil and respectful, add to their dignity, rather than take away from it.

2. Respect your mate's ideas.

When you're living with somebody for ten years, you know where every thought will lead. You look at a news bulletin and you know what the reaction will be. You sit down to discuss and you pretty much know what their answer will be.
But wouldn't it be nice to hear them out occasionally? When people pounce on you, without hearing you out, I for one, don't share much with them.

You soon discover with whom you can be vulnerable. And you soon discover who takes advantage of you if you show any vulnerability. Don't make fun of each other's suggestions. Most of all, if something the other started doesn't work out properly, don't be too quick to rush in with, "I told you so!" The person who initiates has to be brave. And the person who initiates something that is a failure needs encouragement, not derision.

3. Speak politely.
The friendliest of people can be the most volatile in dealing with their own family. A simple rule of thumb is; always speak as politely to your partner as you would to a business friend you were trying to impress.

4. When you have to disagree, do it with dignity.
The tongue is a damaging scalpel. Only criticise if you have the heart to help. There's no need to accuse. It's easy to say: "The electric fire was left on last night." That's far more helpful than to point the accusing finger and shout, "You left the electric fire on last night!"
In marriage, confrontation is always necessary. There is no growth without it. But ask yourself why you're starting the confrontation? Is it to get your own way? Is it to make your partner feel small? Is it to control your partner? Is it to get back at them? Or is it to help them?

5. Respect privacy.
Whenever I assist at a marriage, I like to have the well-known three candle-sermon. Two candles at the beginning to show the two lives who came into the church and a third candle lit to show their new life in the future.
It amazes me to see more priests asking the couples to blow out the two candles which they lit at the beginning of the ceremony. It's as if their lives up to that point are snuffed out now. Nothing could be further from the truth. You still have your own life as well as your life together.
Everybody needs to have space, especially within marriage. Try to have space and time to yourself, and to understand when somebody else needs it.

6. Keep your priorities right.

In marriage, it's easy to get things out of proportion. The faults of your partner eventually will be magnified, so magnified that you won't see the good points. That's what "keeping priorities right" means. When something goes wrong, look at the good things they have done for you and with you that day. Highlight them. Then you'll get the little annoying aspects in proper perspective.

7. Always control your own money.

It's important for a number of reasons. It gives you a sense of independence. It also makes you respect money. It's easy to let him or her look after all the money. It stops you worrying about it. That means they had to do all the worrying.

It also means that they're more likely to do without so that you can have your way. It's a subtle form of bribery to let somebody else control the money.

But what happens if they die or get into financial trouble? You're left helpless. Take responsibility for your money. It gives you a sense of power, a sense of authority, and most of all, a sense of respect and responsibility. And, since most of the time we're worrying about money, a burden shared is a burden halved.

8. Don't settle for a quiet life.

That means we have to make a conscious effort to grow, emotionally, spiritually and intellectually. We have to stretch ourselves frequently. A marriage is improved by attempting to improve it.

It's always distressing to see a woman pouting like a child because she doesn't get her way. It's even worse to see a husband slamming a door or out drinking with the boys because he doesn't get his way.

Try to read some book which helps you emotionally. If necessary, go on courses together. Sometimes go on retreat together. Discuss things. Don't settle for a cosy life, in religion, emotionally or in keeping abreast of current affairs.

9. Keep your love alive.

This is the romantic bit. Don't be afraid to play silly games expressing your love for your partner. It's nice to be a little childish

Ten Tips For Happiness

1. Make up your mind to be happy. Learn to find pleasure in simple things.
2. Make the best of your circumstances. No one has everything and everyone has something of sorrow intermingled with the gladness of life. The trick is to make the laughter outweigh the tears.
3. Don't take yourself too seriously.
4. You can't please everybody. Don't let criticism hurt you.
5. Don't let your neighbours set your standards. Be yourself.
6. Don't borrow trouble. Imaginary things are harder to bear than the actual ones.
7. Since hate poisons the soul, do not cherish enmities or grudges. Avoid people who make you unhappy.
8. Don't spend your life brooding over sorrows or mistakes. Don't be one who never gets over things.
9. Do what you can for those less fortunate than yourself.
10. Keep busy at something. A busy person never has time to be unhappy.

Robert Louis Stevenson (1850 - 1894)

every now and again. Have weekends together. Have nights out together. Have walks together. Hold hands, kiss often and make love as frequently as is meaningful.

Take time to pray together too. You may not like the same form of prayer. But there is something especially beautiful to see a couple coming to church together. It's even nicer to see the whole family come together.

I appreciate that that is not possible for most families. It may not even be possible for a husband and wife to go because of difficult working hours. But find some time to pray together.

10. Treasure your life together.

There will come a time when you'll be separated. There will come a time when you won't have each other. And that's heartbreaking. At this very moment, I suspect widows and widowers throughout the country have just burst into tears. And I've no doubt that many of them will write to me, saying: "You're perfectly right to stress the importance of enjoying each other while you still have each other!"

Life is a fragile thread, and love is an even more fragile one. Both can slip through your fingers without your realising they've even been there.

If I were to sum up what I'd have to say to a couple it would be this: try to share the best moments of your life and your personality and your gifts, with each other.

At the end of your life together you will at least have the wonderful consolation of knowing that you did the best you could and you gave the best you had.

Joe Di Maggio's Lonely Love

I don't know if you'll find this story as sad, as beautiful or as poignant as I do.

Flicking through an American magazine, I found an account of how Joe Di Maggio has spent the 14th of January every year since 1962.

Joe Di Maggio was, in his heyday, the greatest baseball player ever to play for the Yankees and acknowledged to be the most gracious and flamboyant as well.

He's 80 years old now. But he can never forget the ten months he was married to the most famous and most beautiful woman in the world, Marilyn Monroe.

And that is why, on 14th January, the anniversary of their wedding, baseball's most brilliant player goes alone to place two red roses on Marilyn Monroe's grave in Westwood Cemetery, Los Angeles.

Di Maggio, bent and grey now, spends an hour in solitude beside his former wife's marble grave.

They were married in 1954 for a mere ten months. Then they were Mr and Mrs America. And whilst their marriage was a turbulent affair, Di Maggio's passion for the blonde goddess still remains untouched by the passing of almost half a century.

When Marilyn Monroe died in 1962, Di Maggio was the one who arranged and paid for her funeral. He did it so that there would be as little Hollywood glitz as possible. It was he who banned his old drinking companions, Sinatra, Dean Martin and Peter Lawford, as well as anyone remotely connected with the Kennedy family, from attending the memorial service.

This shy, private man, who is almost a recluse now, has never re-married, has never been romantically linked with another woman, and has never spoken publicly of his time with the world's most beautiful woman.

But, for over 30 years, three times a week, red roses have appeared on Marilyn's tombstone. A Beverly Hills florist does it mostly. On special occasions Maggio himself delivers them.

Di Maggio was so special that Paul Simon, in a song from the soundtrack of the Graduate, used him as a symbol of the lost innocence of his youth. "Where have you gone to, Joe Di Maggio? A nation turns its lonely eyes on you."

Paul Simon was a New York Yankee fan from boyhood. And he explained why he wrote those lines when he said: "Our boyhood heroes are special. They are people who are all good and have no bad in them at all. That's the way I always saw Joe Di Maggio."

Di Maggio first met Marilyn Monroe shortly after he retired from the game in 1951.

He saw a publicity picture of her for *Clash By Night*, and was so smitten that even though he was a mature man of 38 at the time, he called the studio boss personally to arrange a blind date at one of Hollywood's restaurants with Monroe.

Marilyn knew nothing about baseball, nor about the legend with whom she was dining. She arrived two hours late. And her interest in Di Maggio was only kindled when Mickey Rooney, in the same restaurant, came over for an autograph — not from Monroe but from Di Maggio.

Fifteen months later they were married and the celebrated telegram from May West arrived: "Love and congratulations. But Marilyn, why marry one ball player when you could have had the whole team?"

Marilyn signed the register, Norma Jean Dougherty, her real name.

Sadly, it was not a marriage to last. It was made in Hollywood, not in heaven.

Di Maggio, mature as he was, thought that Marilyn would be happy to abandon her movie career.

That was something she could not do.

He liked to live a relatively anonymous life.

She liked to hang out with the movie crowd.

And as each picture of her became more sexy and she became more famous, Di Maggio's disillusionment grew.

They separated finally during the filming of *The Seven Year Itch*.

Di Maggio visited the set and during the famous scene in which Marilyn's dress flies up while standing over a New York subway grating, Di Maggio was furious to see his wife revealing her underwear.

The scene was shot over and over until it was perfect. The crowds got bigger and bigger. And Di Maggio became increasingly humiliated.

That night they had a row in the hotel which became a very public affair, mainly because of breaking glass and splintering wood.

On hearing of the break-up, a comedian is supposed to have said: "It just goes to show, no man can be an expert at our two national pastimes."

Marilyn, as they say, went from bad to worse. Di Maggio became a recluse but never forgot.

And that is why this dignified sporting giant spends a silent hour in prayer beside the grave of the only woman he ever loved.

Had she realised the depth of his love she might not be in that grave.

To Live Is To Risk

To laugh is to risk appearing the fool.
To weep is to risk appearing sentimental.
To reach out for another is to risk involvement.
To expose feelings is to risk exposing your true self.
To place your ideas, your dreams, before the crowd is to
risk their loss.
To love is to risk not being loved in return.
To live is to risk dying.
To hope is to risk despair.
To try at all is to risk failure.
But risk we must. Because the greatest hazard to life is
to risk nothing.
The person who risks nothing has nothing, does nothing, is
nothing.
They may avoid suffering and sorrow, but they simply
cannot learn, feel, change, grow, love, live.
Chained by their certitudes they are slaves; they have
forfeited freedom.
Only the person who risks can be called free — and
only someone who is free can be called a child of God.

Anything Goes Because Nothing Matters

There is a great deal of cant about pornography.

There is no doubt that pornography is harmful. It damages those who create it and those who use it. It diminishes human dignity and mutilates all of us sometimes more than we recognise.

When it victimises children it is at its most horrific.

Pornography has been around a long time. They say it was scratched on the walls of caves.

But pornography is not the only problem. Pornography is also the result of another problem. It seems to me that all our troubles begin when there is sex with no sense of the sacred.

Too often, what passes for Church teaching falls into the same trap as pornography. It talks about sex in an abstract and wholly inhuman way. Like pornography it tends to strip sex of the sacred.

It's part of a modern malaise. Listen to people talking. Have you noticed that nobody falls in love any more? They have "a relationship." Hardly anyone "makes love." But they are obsessed with "having sex."

Courtship is a dirty word. And for many, marriage is no longer a truly romantic adventure. It's more like a court room battle over contracts and commitments, territory and power.

Talk shows seem to thrive on imprudent people being willing to blab like idiots about intimate details of their love life.

It's a question of "Anything goes, because nothing matters."

It's sex with no sense of the sacred.

And so sex is mechanistic, amoral, easy, inhuman — without love and without dignity.

We need more of love and less about sex.

What for example does the Church say these days to single people? I'll talk about the Catholic Church specifically on this matter.

If you were to put all the statements about sex and the single Catholic in a book I'm afraid it would be a rather slim volume.

It so happens that I've been caught in the middle of a few very heated discussions on that subject in my time.

There was a time when sex and the single Catholic referred mainly to couples going out before they were married or to some person who decided not go get married.

John B. Keane's *The Chastitude* made me feel very uncomfortable because so much of it is so true.

But times have changed. A woman I spoke with recently was divorced. She had been married for 19 years to a man who abused her because of his addiction to alcohol.

The marriage was difficult but what lies ahead of her now is equally painful. In her view the rules have changed. When she got married she was a conservative 21-year-old petrified virgin. Everything was clear. She didn't have to make any decisions. Now she faces a new set of decisions.

As a result it took her three years before she felt comfortable enough to date someone. And when you hear a 45-year-old woman with a lot of experience say: "I don't think God is all that concerned about responsible adults fulfilling their sexual needs; what He is concerned with is violence, crime, poverty, drugs, abuse and damaging human beings," you listen carefully and make suggestions tentatively.

She is totally against indiscriminate sex but sees something different for mature adults who have reached a mutual decision after a lot of discussion.

One of her friends who is slightly older and in a similar position had an even stronger view.

She didn't see sex as a temptation or an act of falling away from God. "I don't think I need to beg God's forgiveness for making love," she said. "I don't carry around a lot of guilt regarding sexual experiences I have had because I believe it to be a responsible decision."

The basis of her view is that sex between two caring adults is an expression of love. It's an integral part of sharing, loving relationship.

She said that those people who don't have full-time partners and aren't making babies ought to have a home in the Church.

So how's the Church going to make them feel at home?

There has been some growth in moral matters. When I was first ordained, if you were understanding about birth control there was always a long queue outside your confessional. It was, for many, the only sin.

I hear just as many confessions nowadays. But I rarely hear anyone mentioning contraception.

That seems to me to say that Catholics are looking at the Church's teaching and making up their own minds on how those teachings fit their lives.

If you want a grown-up Church you have to start treating your people like grown-ups and stop treating them like juveniles.

The Church has the right and the duty to teach clearly and compassionately about sex, sexuality, marriage and morality in general. But passion being what it is, people will come to their own conclusions about the use of their sexuality.

Does that make them bad people? That's not up to me to judge. That's up to God.

Suffering From Solutions

Peter and Jim were partners in a profitable painting contracting business but unfortunately, they were not entirely honest. They diluted the paint with lashings of turpentine.

One day Jim's conscience started to bother him as they painted a poor widow's house.

The next day Jim told Peter he just could not go on being dishonest any more.

"Don't quit now," Peter begged. "A few more years like this and we can retire."

But Jim refused to change his mind.

"Peter", he said, "I just cannot do it. Last night an angel came to me and sat beside my bed and said to me: REPAINT YOU THINNER."

Happiness Is ...

A man found a magic lantern and, for years, every time he rubbed it a "Genie" would appear to grant his wish.

Because of his constant anxious worries, the man kept "Genie" busy. This went on for years - one wish after another - until one day the "Genie" appeared and said;

"I am sick and tired of your anxious worry and your constant wishing. I have decided to settle this arrangement we have, once and for all. I will grant your next three wishes and nothing more. After that you're on your own."

The man made his first wish immediately. He asked that his wife would disappear so that he could marry another woman.

His wish came true.

But when friends and relatives discovered she was gone they began to recall all the wife's good qualities. This saddened the man and he realised he had been hasty.

Where would he find a better woman than his wife?

So, he asked "Genie" to bring her back and immediately his wish was granted.

Now he had but one wish left.

He fretted and agonised about that third wish. He was determined not to make another mistake, since he would be unable to correct it. He went everywhere for advice.

Some people told him to wish for immortality. But if he got sick, he reasoned, what good would immortality be?

"Maybe", he told himself, "I should wish for good health." But then he asked himself: "What good is health if I don't have much money? And what good is money if I have no friends?"

Many years passed and still he worried.

Finally, in desperation, he cried out: "Someone tell me what to ask for!"

And he heard a gentle voice from within answer: "Ask to be content, no matter what you get."

They say that happiness is not a destination, but rather a manner of travelling. Happiness is not an end in itself, but a by-product of working, playing, loving and living.

A good example of this is the story of a young man who went to a psychologist for help after he changed his mind about committing suicide.

He had planned to jump off a bridge but was stopped by a very simple act. While driving his car to the bridge he stopped at a traffic light. Looking towards the side-walk he spotted an elderly woman smiling at him. He felt himself smiling back.

That light changed and he drove on. But the memory of that simple smile stayed with him.

Later he told the psychologist: "Her smile made me think that perhaps I wasn't so bad after all."

Never underestimate the power of simple things and never underestimate the power of a smile.

We need to encourage one another. In his youth Thomas Edison, the great inventor, struggled with serious learning disabilities.

After only three months at school he returned home one day in tears because his teacher had called him stupid and put him at the back of the class.

When Edison's mother learned what had happened she confronted the teacher. Then she took her son out of the school and taught him herself at home.

There she nurtured his natural curiosity.

Many years later Edison said of his mother: "Her encouragement helped me to believe in myself."

Encouragement of those around you not only brightens their future but brightens your own as well.

None of us controls everything in life. But we can make choices about who we are and what we do. Today choose to be the person God had in mind when He chose to create you.

An elderly religious called Brother Jeremiah was once asked what he would do differently if he had his life to live again. This is his reply:

"If I had my life over again, I'd try to make more mistakes next time. I would limber up. I would be sillier than I have been this trip. I would take more trips, I would climb more mountains, swim more rivers, and watch more sunsets. I would do more walking and looking. I would have more actual troubles and fewer imaginary ones...

"Oh, I've had my moment and if I had it to do over again, I'd have more of them. In fact, I'd try to have nothing else. Just moments, one after another, instead of living so many years ahead of each day...

"If I had my life to live over, I would start barefooted earlier in the spring and stay that way later in the autumn. I would play truant more. I would ride more merry-go-rounds. I'd pick more daisies." (Brother Jeremiah)

Had these words been written by a young person, they would not have the same power. There's something within youth that, more naturally, seizes the moment.

Unfortunately, much of that spirit dies as the burdens of duty weigh us down.

Sadly, I suspect that most of us will have very similar sentiments to Brother Jeremiah when we look back on our lives. It's always too late when we realise how seldom we really *lived*.

Just The Ticket!

The perplexed clergyman could not find a parking space for his car. He eventually parked on double yellow lines and left the following note under the wiper.

Dear Traffic Warden,
I've been around the block ten times and couldn't find a vacant parking space. "Forgive us our trespasses."

Yours faithfully,
Rev George.

He returned a half hour later and found a reply along with a parking ticket.

Dear Rev,
I've been around the block for ten years. "Lead us not into temptation."

Yours sincerely,
Your friendly Traffic Warden.

The Amazing Story of Sojourner Truth

Sojourner Truth was born at the end of the 18th century and sold into slavery at the age of ten. She was an amazing woman who fought battles for women long before it was fashionable.

She was owned by a Dutch slave-master in the state of New York. Like all slaves then, she had to take the name of the owner as her own.

She gave birth to 13 children, every one of whom in turn was sold into slavery across America. She had no say in the matter.

When her owner thought that the slave was nearing the end of her life, she was given her freedom and at once she changed her name.

She said that she always felt called by God to pursue truth and she now wanted to spend the rest of her life journeying around, helping, encouraging and, in some cases, cajoling people to seek freedom for slaves and civil rights for women — in general the pursuit of truth.

She took the name *Sojourner Truth*.

In fact, she lived to be over 80, travelled America, became extremely famous and did much good.

There are many stories about her. Once she was asked to preach in a Baptist church in the Deep South. A throng of admirers came to hear what she had to say.

But the elders of the church felt a little uneasy when they met her. She was a huge, big, woman, over six feet tall. Her demeanour was masculine, her voice deep and resonant. Added to which, she incessantly smoked a foul-smelling, oversized pipe.

Quietly the elders wondered if this was indeed the real Sojourner. Was she someone out to trick them? Was she a woman at all?

So, they hit on a plan which they put to Sojourner as diplomatically as possible. They suggested that the lady's committee would meet her privately in a room at the back and carry out their own discreet investigation. When they were satisfied that Sojourner was a woman they would be delighted to hear her preach.

But Sojourner was not to be doubted.

There and then, she ripped open her blouse and in her best bass voice said: "These breasts of mine have suckled many children of white people. They have given life and milk to white children, children who should have been given milk by their own mothers, children who were fed at my breasts when my own children were left hungry and crying. If you still doubt me, come and try them yourself."

Sojourner preached.

On another occasion, some of her friends were anxious about her smoking. They were not too happy about the smell from the pipe or, for that matter, the indignity of a famous woman smoking a pipe at all.

A friend said gently: "Sojourner, you know that you are a venerable lady now. We hope you don't die for many years and we are sure you won't. Yet, you should be careful.

"All this pipe smoking is not good for you and if you don't stop smoking it could be that the Good Lord will be none too happy to let you into heaven with the awful breath you have from that stinking pipe."

Sojourner took the pipe from her mouth and spat out: "Friends, when I goes to the Good Lord, I sure as hell intend to leave my breath behind me here. I knows the Good Lord won't have to deal with that problem."

She once came uninvited to a rally which was demanding equal voting rights for women in Ohio in 1852.

Many of the more genteel were hoping she wouldn't come at all. They were astounded when she charged into the meeting.

As she arrived, there were many clergymen, as usual, arguing against the practical implications of the equality of women. One was just explaining how the Lord chose twelve apostles and none of them was a woman.

"If the Lord wanted women to be equal he would have chosen some women amongst them. And of course it was of no small import that the Good Lord was, in any case, a man himself."

Sojourner did not wait to be invited but gave a long speech outlining her own life and that of other women. She finished with the immortal reminder:

"As you say, the Good Lord was indeed a man. But when the Good Lord came to be made man, it was arranged between God and woman. And man had nothing to do with it.

"If the first woman God ever made was strong enough to turn the world upside-down all alone, together women ought to be able to turn it right-side-up again."

Love And Hisses

It was the title, "The Snake That Poisons", in The Wall Street Journal, *which caught my attention.*
This is what it said.
It topples governments, wrecks marriages, ruins careers,
busts reputations, causes heartaches, nightmares,
indigestion: it spins suspicion, generates grief, dispatches
innocent people to cry on their pillows.
Even its name hisses. It's called gossip.
There's office gossip, shop gossip, party gossip.
It makes headlines and headaches.
Before you repeat a story, ask yourself three questions.
Is it true?
Is it fair?
Is it necessary?
If not, shut up.

Why You Should Make Love

I hope you'll be able to sympathise with this woman's predicament. The letter was obviously written in haste and with an obvious amount of justifiable anger.

"I'd like to know is there anyone out there who can identify with me?" she began.

"I'm married for 19 years. The first 14 were happy.

"We made friends with this other married couple who are well known to us. My husband became withdrawn, secretive, told lies and eventually hit the bottle. Everything seemed to vanish over-night.

"I became suspicious of his late nights and phone calls behind my back.

"I confided all this to a woman friend of ours. I found her a good listener. About six months later my world fell apart, when all and sundry began talking about the affair my husband was having with my so-called woman friend.

"They were seen after midnight in all kinds of places. I got phone calls 'to open my eyes'.

"At this stage I didn't know who the woman was. And then a true friend told me and I could not believe it.

"I followed him a few nights and sure enough I saw with my own eyes what traitors they were.

"It's gone from bitterness to hate. My husband was violent when I confronted him and she avoided me in every way possible.

"I was the mother of four teenage children and it came to the stage when I could no longer live under the same roof as him. I packed my bags and left. To the day I die I will never forgive either of those two.

"One who was my partner for better or worse until death do us part and the other a woman who visited my home and took away all my happiness leaving a family devastated.

"I'm going through a separation and I hope the future holds a peaceful path for me.

"I would never have anything to do with a man again.

"Whatever the future holds for those two is their own business. All I want is to try to rebuild my life. I hope and pray God will guide me to take one day at a time and to regain my confidence. I hope I have the courage to face life with dignity and try to bury the bad years.

"Most of all I pray for my family who have to start out in life and to suffer the frustration of having their home broken up at a young age.

"I don't feel guilty about the steps I've taken since I wasn't the one who did wrong.

"It seems to me marriage for some is a farce.

"One quotation I heard as a child was, 'If you burn yourself sit on the blister.'

"But if the blister isn't self-inflicted, why should anyone sit on it? Beware of those who befriend you, they could wreck your life."

Signed: Disillusioned

That's a most difficult and sad case. It happens so frequently. And there is so much bitterness.

But bitterness kills and there is no life until it is dealt with. You simply have to get help and work a painful path through it.

It just so happens that, when I got the letter I was reading a piece by Dr. Jack Dominian, who is one of the leading authorities on marriage and sexuality. He always talks a great deal of practical sense.

What caught my eye this time was his view on affairs, marriages and love. He thinks, after many years as an experienced counsellor, that an affair is a complex phenomenon and is often much more than the pursuit of sex.

Often the man pursues an affair extra-maritally for sex and the woman for affection. And, according to Dr. Dominian, adultery is common.

It is estimated that 60% of men and 40% of women in Britain will have an affair and sometimes more than one.

Dr. Dominian says: "An affair is an attack on the mutual trust of the couple and hurts deeply. But it is never a black-and-white episode."

"The person who commits the adultery is considered the culprit, but one has to reflect on what was missing from the relationship in order to have encouraged the affair," Dr. Dominian argues.

"Thus adultery is not an automatic reason for a divorce or marital breakdown. What is needed is good and honest communication to find out what is missing from the relationship and to try to restore it."

He says that sexual intercourse ought to sustain a couple and offer a healing growth to each other as well. Intercourse must always be linked with loving.

The sexual act is a body language through which the couple talk to each other. And when they do, they say at least five things.

"The first thing they say is: 'You are the most important person in my life; I recognise you; I want you and I appreciate you.' In other words they reaffirm each other's importance.

"Secondly, in making love the man makes the woman feel most completely feminine and the woman makes the man most completely masculine.

"In this way they affirm each other's sexual identity.

"Thirdly, as we have seen, couples argue and quarrel. A relationship can be strained. They could be temporarily alienated and drift apart.

"After a little while when they come together again and make love, it is a sign of reconciliation."

"Fourthly, we all want meaning in life. If one knows that every few days the most important person in your life wants you, the sexual act becomes a sign of hope.

"And, finally, sexual intercourse becomes an act of thanksgiving. It is a way of saying thank you for being with me yesterday, today and hopefully tomorrow."

Dr. Dominian says that, seen this way, sexual intercourse is an act which gives life to the couple and indeed can give new life to their relationship.

"It is the central act of prayer of the sacrament which revitalises the rest of marriage."

He maintains that, generally speaking, a man wants to make love on many occasions to release sexual tension. This is determined hormonally and a wife ought to understand and respond to it.

The wife, on the other hand, wants sexual intercourse in a setting of affection and the husband ought to ensure that it is always preceded and followed by tenderness and care.

"In this way every act as far as possible meets the needs of both partners," he concludes.

I know what I've written here won't help "Disillusioned" too much, but it could help others to avoid the heartache, the bitterness and the trauma she, her children and some others who are less obvious, have suffered.

You Are Beautiful

Treat yourself the way you are, and you will remain so.
Treat yourself the way you can become, and you will become so.
Think freely. Smile often.
Tell those you love that you do.
Hope, grow, give, give in.
Pick some daisies. Keep a promise.
Laugh heartily. Enjoy. Trust life.
Reach out. Let someone in.
Make some mistakes. Learn from them.
Explore the unknown. Believe in yourself.
Celebrate your life! *You are beautiful.*

Helping A Loved One With Aids To Die

I remember for the first time I went to a morgue to say prayers for a young man who had died from an Aids-related illness. The shock was terrible.

Three days before, I had been with the young man in the last moments of his life.

By then I was not afraid to touch him, be with him and respect him.

But in the morgue I couldn't see a body. The body was wrapped in a black plastic sack.

It was in America and it shocked me. Sometimes things don't change all that much.

With all the bad publicity given to people suffering from Aids, misunderstandings are inevitable.

So if you know someone with Aids, here are a few tips, from those involved in the ministry, on how you might behave.

First of all, you need to know what you're dealing with. If you're afraid of contracting Aids from being near a person, then you can't be yourself.

We don't know everything about Aids at the present time, but we do know that you have nothing to fear by being physically close to a person with Aids. You can sit in the same room, you can eat dinner with the person, you can drink tea from the same cup. You can kiss, you can hug. The Aids virus is not airborne. It's transmitted by direct contact with an infected person's bodily fluids, most notably blood and semen.

It's no harm to admit you're scared. In fact, if you try to mask your fear it won't work. Somebody close to you will pick up your attitudes. They'll notice the look in your eye. They'll notice the nervousness of your touch.

If you need to talk it over with somebody in the caring profession or a trusted friend or a counsellor, then do it. But don't carry your fears and prejudices into the room with you.

And most of us, despite our best efforts, do carry fears and prejudices.

If the person with Aids is a homosexual or if they have contracted it through IV drug abuse, then you'll have certain feelings about homosexuality and drug abuse which you'll carry into that sick room.

But remember that Aids is a disease, not a moral issue. It is an indiscriminate disease. It can and does strike people without regard to age, background, lifestyle or vocation. I've been in a room with a person dying from an Aids-related illness, one of whom was a priest and the other a joyrider, bag snatcher and drug addict. And both of them died beautiful deaths.

So if you're going to be in a room with somebody dying from an Aids-related illness, look beyond the way the person contracted the disease. See the human being dying. This will help you overcome or at least set aside the prejudice you have about Aids.

When we go into the room of anybody who's near death we have two major problems to overcome. First of all, we have our emotions about the person dying. And even more importantly, we have to overcome our own fear of death. Aids is no different. It forces us to come face to face with the certainty of our loved one's death and face to face with out own mortality.

No-one gets out of this world alive. Life is a terminal illness yet this is a strange death-denying culture we live in. We're uncomfortable with the fact of death. If you try to be honest about your own fears of death you'll be more at peace with someone who, at this moment, just happens to be a little further along the journey.

If you're particularly close to the person dying, you have a different set of emotions to cope with. You go through many of the same emotions the dying person goes through. You try to deny it. You bargain with God. You'll go through the many stages of grief.

So you need to pay attention to your own feelings.

It's essential to realise that when someone you love hurts, you'll hurt too. And if you put all your energy into trying to be strong even when you feel anything but strong, you'll not have any energy left to help the person you love.

You have to have a way of expressing your own grief. Normally that means looking for someone other than the person with Aids to help you through your own sorrow.

To be good for the person dying with Aids you need to find strength from some other person or group.

Nobody walks through the stages of grief in easy and tidy steps. Grieving is a messy business. If you allow yourself to experience your feelings fully, however uncomfortable that may be at the time, you will allow healing into your life.

The best way to help somebody dying with Aids is to be there with them. People with Aids often experience isolation. There is still a stigma that continues to surround the disease. They are shunned. People in the health-care business who should know better shun them and so do many of their loved ones.

If you want to be there for the person it's not just a question of time nor even being in their presence physically. It's a matter of a gentle and healing presence. If you are dealing with your own brokenness you will find that you are a worthwhile companion. If you're suppressing your own brokenness then it doesn't matter how much time you spend there, you'll merely add to the confusion of the dying person.

You don't need to fuss over them like a mother hen. You don't need to remind them that they should rest more and eat more and shouldn't be going out. It's just better to allow a person to live the time they have to the fullest and in the way they enjoy it best.

If you're particularly close to the person, the hardest thing you'll have to do is to let go. That doesn't mean abandoning them. It means that their life is not yours to control. You can't save your loved one from Aids. You can, though, be a source of comfort, strength and hope.

I remember a young man dying of Aids telling me that, because his mother wanted him to be well, he was forced to hide his illness from her. He tried to hide what was happening to him so that those closest to him wouldn't feel the pain.

Ultimately "letting go" means that the one you love belongs to a Higher Power. Turn the person over to the care of that Higher Power through prayer and you'll be one step nearer peace to you both. There is a freedom in being a companion to your loved one while he or she is still with you.

You need to be grateful too. Don't misunderstand me. I don't mean that you should be grateful for Aids. Aids is a devastating disease that we must fight with all the resources we can. But in almost every curse there's a blessing.

People with Aids, like any person near to death, can teach us a lot about living. They can tell us about the value of daily living.

Often people with Aids tell me that it has been a blessing to them too. They can look at life differently. They are able to forgive. They can mend fences. They learn about themselves. Each day is a blessing simply because they have got through another day. And most of them know that when death comes it will bring the ultimate healing.

So be aware of what the person with Aids is telling you. About death. About life. About companionship and compassion. About faith and hope.

Not hope for a miracle cure, though we all hope and pray that that day will soon come. But hope that no life is wasted. And that if we live our life on this earth to the full there is a better life awaiting us.

In the last analysis, it's love, not Aids, which conquers all.

Giving and Living

A rich man asked a friend why he was always criticised for being so miserly.

"Everyone knows I will leave everything to charity when I die," he argued.

"Well," said the friend, "let me tell you the story about the pig and the cow. The pig was lamenting to the cow one day about how unhappy he was. 'People are always talking about your gentleness and your kind eyes,' said the pig to the cow. 'We know you give milk and cream, but I give more. I give bacon and ham. They pickle my feet, still nobody likes me. Why is this?"

"The cow thought for a minute and then replied: 'Maybe it's because I give when I'm still living'."

A Crabbed Old Woman

*These verses were found by a nurse among the possessions
of an old woman who had died.*

What do you see, nurse, what do you see?
What are you thinking when you are looking at me -
A crabbit old woman, not very wise,
Uncertain of habit, with faraway eyes.

Who dribbles her food and makes no reply
When you say in a loud voice: "I do wish you'd try"
Who seems not to notice the things that you do.
And forever is losing a stocking or shoe.

Who unresisting or not, lets you do as you will
With bathing and feeding, the long day to fill.
Is that what you're thinking, is that what you see?
Then open your eyes, nurse, you're not looking at me.

I'll tell you who I am as I sit here so still,
As I rise at your bidding, as I eat at your will,
I'm a small child of ten with a father and mother,
Brothers and sisters who love one another.

A young girl of sixteen with wings on her feet,
Dreaming that soon now a lover she'll meet,
A bride soon at twenty, my heart gives a leap,
Remembering the vows that I promised to keep;

At twenty-five now I have young of my own,
Who need me to build a secure happy home;
A woman of thirty, my young now grow fast,
Bound to each other with ties that should last.

At forty, my young sons have grown and have gone,
But my man's beside me to see I don't mourn;
At fifty once more babies play round my knee,
Again we know children, my loved one and me.

Dark days are upon me, my husband is dead,
I look at the future, I shudder with dread,
For my young are all rearing young of their own,
And I think of the years and the love that I've known.

I'm an old woman now and nature is cruel,
'Tis her jest to make old age look like a fool.
The body it crumbles, grace and vigour depart;
There is now a stone where I once had a heart.

But inside this old carcass a young girl still dwells,
And now and again my battered heart swells,
I remember the joys, I remember the pain,
And I'm loving and living life over again.

I think of the years all too few gone too fast.
And accept the stark fact that nothing can last.
So open your eyes, nurse, open and see,
Not a crabbit old woman look close — see ME!

The Nurse's Reply

What do we see, you ask, what do we see?
Yes, we are thinking when looking at thee!
We may seem to be hard when we hurry and fuss,
But there's many of you and too few of us.

We would like far more time to sit by you and talk,
To bath you and feed you and help you to walk.
To hear of your lives and the things you have done,
Your childhood, your husband, your daughter, your son.

But time is against us — there's too much to do,
Patients too many and nurses too few.
We grieve when we see you, no friends of your own;
We feel all your pain and we know of your fear
That nobody cares now your end is so near.

But nurses are people with feelings as well,
And when we're together you'll often hear tell
Of the dearest old gran in the very end bed,
And the lovely old dad and the things that he said.

We speak with compassion and love and feel sad,
When we think of your lives and the joys that you've had.
When the time has arrived for you to depart,
You leave us behind with an ache in our heart.

When you sleep the long sleep, no more worry or care,
There are other old people and we must be there.
So, please understand if we hurry and fuss
There are many of you and too few of us...

Superstition

A man named Joe was a superstitious gambler who found
deep meaning in numbers. He was born on April 4th and
was 44 years old. He had four children and lived at 444
West 4th Street. During the past 4 years he earned $44,000
a year as a manager at the corporate headquarters of
The Four Brothers Pizza Chain.
On his 44th birthday, he went to the dog track and was
surprised that a dog named Lucky 44 was running in the
fourth race. Four minutes before the race began, he went to
the fourth window and plonked down $4,000 on number 4.
And sure enough, the dog finished fourth.

F.W. de Klerk: A Man For All Seasons

The most suprisingly likeable and wise man on the political front in South Africa was a man I'd previously had little respect for — the former President and now Deputy President, F.W. de Klerk.

As a disciple of apartheid, Frederick Willem de Klerk had impeccable credentials.

He came from a prominent Afrikaner family, which had ruled South Africa since 1948. His father, Jan, served as a cabinet minister under Hendrik Verwoerd, the architect of apartheid, whose schemes were designed to rid South Africa of all blacks and ensure white supremacy.

His uncle, J.G. Strydom, was a former Prime Minister and a bigot.

Earlier generations had a solid Afrikaner history. De Klerk was steeped in the traditions of Afrikaner politics and history.

His own career followed a predicable course. He took a leading role in student affairs at the Afrikaner university in Potchesfstroom, set up a successful law practice in staunch Vereeniging and lived by the strict Calvinist traditions of the Dutch Reform Church — the church which for decades taught that the religious justification of apartheid was contained in the Bible.

De Klerk entered Parliament in 1978 and at the age of 42 became the youngest member of John Vorster's cabinet.

He conformed faithfully to the Nationalist Party and all that it stood for.

He spoke adamantly against integrated sports, mixed race marriages, trade union rights for blacks and black claims for permanent residence in South Africa.

And he was the strongest defender of the policy to keep whites, blacks, coloureds and Indians in separate areas, by law.

As late as 1989, de Klerk said: "Whites must be guaranteed a community life, their own areas, schools, institutions and systems..."

So when the time came for the Nationalist Party to choose a successor to P.W. Botha in 1989, de Klerk was the favoured candidate of the right-wing members.

But from the vantage point of the President's office, de Klerk saw a different picture.

It began with a religious experience during his inauguration. He invited his favourite pastor to preach at the service.

Taking his text from Jeremiah 23, the clergyman told the new President that he "was standing in the council chamber of God" to learn the will of God, and that he should act upon it.

As God's instrument, the preacher said, the new leader should heed the traditions of his people, but should also have the courage to break new ground.

de Klerk was deeply affected by the pastor's words.

At the end of the service he asked his family to pray for him. He told them he knew now that he would be rejected by his own people, but that he was chosen to walk this road and they must help him.

He later spoke about the service: "I felt a strong sense of calling, not in an arrogant way, as though I felt I was being looked upon as somebody special who had been singled out by God Almighty to do this job. But I was and am very conscious of my shortcomings and I constantly try to overcome them.

"I do believe that God directs things on earth, and as a result I had to accept that God wanted my election and I must realise that in my actions, I have a responsibility to God. No matter what I do down here, I will have to answer to God. I try to live according to that."

And there is no doubt he did take many initiatives which led to the dismantling of the horrible apartheid system.

Once in the President's office, he soon realised that, since 1985 particularly, South Africa was governable only as a "state of emergency".

Abroad, South Africa was regarded as a pariah state, shunned by all respectable countries and subjected to trade sanctions and sports boycotts.

Foreign bankers refused to give new loans and scores of major corporations pulled out of the country.

From its base in Lusaka, the African National Congress was committed to bringing down the apartheid state by revolutionary war and was well positioned to do so.

Against that background, de Klerk could either do as his

predecessors did, rule by ever more heavy-handed repression, or he could try to give blacks a rightful voice in their own country.

In fact he had little choice. Inspiration may have helped him to move, but the stark facts spoke very loudly too.

To his credit, he began discussions. He was, and still is, rejected by many Afrikaners as a traitor, and he suffered greatly.

Not even he, though, knew what a can of worms he was opening.

He never intended to give any power or to concede "one man one vote."

He had no idea that he would end up a mere deputy President.

Once he had set himself on the road to reform, though, he battled gamely on.

And that is why I believe him to be a politician of conviction, who deserves respect and who is an essential to a peaceful South Africa as Nelson Mandela is.

The temptation for de Klerk to back off, to keep his privileged position, to lead his people down the "Afrikaners say No road", must have been great.

He didn't do it.

He was shrewd enough to acknowledge that the world had changed and that a peaceful solution would demand sacrifices.

The bottom line is this: When it came to taking the painful road to peace, it was de Klerk who had to make the longest journey.

For whatever reason, he made that journey and still makes it to this day.

Three Questions

This is a lesson about money.
A man asked a lawyer what his fee was.
"I charge £50 for answering three questions,"
the lawyer answered.
"That's awfully steep, isn't it?" the man asked.
"Yes", replied the lawyer. "Now what's your final
question?"

A Better Relationship Or A Broken Heart?

There are hundreds of books on "How to have a better relationship". I've read them. I have a few tips which might help save your marriage, the warning signs you should look for, and even what to do when the relationship breaks up.

For example, they've discovered now that where you were born in the family is of vital importance as to how you relate. If you were born first in the family and you marry someone who was born last in the family, it can be a recipe for disaster.

Eldest children are usually serious adults. They are high achievers who like to do things in a precise way and give themselves ulcers in the process.

Middle children are good negotiators, independent, flexible and sociable.

Young children tend to be charming adults. They are good at getting others to do things for them. They are easy-going and creative.

Only children are used to working to please adults all the time. They are usually stubborn.

Once you understand that, you are most likely to understand your partner's behaviour. You are less likely to see it as a plot against you.

Learning to listen is a skill that can save trouble too. The first rule in learning to listen is simple: look as if you are listening. Don't fidget while someone is talking to you. Don't watch television out of the corner of your eye.

Realise that both men and women have emotions. Women are not just home-makers, and men are not just walking wallets.

When your partner is explaining to you how he or she feels, try to make a mental list of the words they are searching for — *sad, isolated, afraid, exhausted, discouraged, important, happy.* Now set aside time for listening. Twenty minutes a week could save a marriage.

Love and sex can cause problems, as you well know. A lot of women believe that if their husbands loved them, they would know how they feel. Women often expect men to be mind-readers. He thinks she doesn't want to make love because she has turned against him. And so, he mentally breaks off the marriage there and then. She thinks that all he ever thinks about is sex— "If he loved me, he'd understand me better."

The truth, of course may be that he is looking for physical comfort because he got a ticking off from the boss. She is unresponsive because she knows she should have washed her hair and is feeling tired and unattractive. If they had explained that to each other it would have been fine.

There are other simple rules too. Make sure you spend time together. One of the main reasons for marriages breaking up is that couples don't spend enough time with each other.

Support each other when one of you is going through a bad patch. Money problems, illness, the loss of a parent — all can cause stress to one of the partners, and how the other reacts makes a lasting impression on a marriage.

Don't let work or hobbies take priorities in your relationship. Your partner must not be made to feel excluded.

Before having children, know how you would like your children to turn out. That will determine what kind of disipline you should have and what kind of education they are to get.

Don't take your partner for granted. Make them feel special and wanted. Tell them you love them. Show them you love them.

Don't cut off your friends. Keep in touch with a good circle of people you can go out together with.

Marriage is built on love, trust, and feeling special towards another person. Try to make that person feel special all the time, just as you did at the beginning of your relationship.

In short, sharing and caring are still the keys to togetherness.

Yet no matter how hard you try, your relationship may fall apart.

So what do you do to mend a broken heart?

You'll drive yourself nuts if you hang on to a love which has run its course. It is soul-destroying and self-destructive. You'll spend your life in a neurotic way.

You phone, hoping for a friendly word. You spend lonely nights thinking of happier times and, when you finally fall asleep, tainted love invades your dreams. Songs, pictures, places and food trigger your emotions. Your ex-mate takes over your life. Life is a misery which tears your heart out.

People on the rebound find it difficult to settle. So what do you do?

All the best advice is that the end of a relationship deserves a funeral. It deserves a period of grief. They say that you must organise a funeral of everything that reminds you of the romance.

Throw out the gifts, the letters. Learn to have fresh thoughts. Don't be caught staying in, having lonely nights.

Begin by planning nights out. Be kind to yourself. Make new friends and look up old ones to be with you at home. Take up exercise, learn to relax, and you'll get through the hours alone. Each night you endure, you will become more confident.

Thought-blocking is another good idea. Each time you think about what they've done to you, shout in your mind: "STOP!"

Stick a STOP sign on your phone too, to make you stop phoning them. Ask yourself: "What will I gain from calling? How much more rejection have I to endure?"

Take up a hobby or a sport that will divert your attention. Keep an emotional diary. Every day pour out exactly how you feel onto the paper.

Write out your true feelings. Take time off to pour out your anger onto the paper, but make sure nobody sees it. It helps you to release your anger in a harmless way, and forces you to recognise what you feel and why you are angry.

After you have been dumped in love, you always feel inferior, so make a list of your own good points and your ex's bad points. Read it when you think how wonderful he or she was!

The most common and dangerous reaction to heartbreak is to binge on drink or drugs or food. You think it will numb the pain. It doesn't. It only makes you more depressed as you get fat and suffer hangovers.

Be on your guard against convincing yourself that you can handle what you are taking and that you are not addicted. Monitor your food and your drink and your drug-intake by writing it down.

Best of all, find a friend you can talk to. Not a friend that you are looking to start a new relationship with. Just someone who listens and understands.

There will come a day when you know you are over your heartbreak. It'll be the day when you have loads of energy for enjoying yourself instead of feeling drained. The day when you can honestly thank your lucky stars the relationship ended. The day when you can think of lost love and not be crippled by bitterness.

Slow Me Down Lord.

Slow me down, Lord.
Ease the pounding of my heart by the quieting of my mind.
Steady my hurried pace with a vision of the eternal reach of time.
Give me, amid the confusion of the day,
The calmness of the everlasting hills.

Break the tensions of my nerves and muscles
With the soothing music of the singing streams that live in my memory.
Help me to know the magical, restoring power of sleep.

Teach me the art of taking minute vacations,
Of slowing down to look at a flower,
To chat with a friend, to pat a dog,
To read a few lines from a good book.

Slow me down, Lord, and inspire me
To send my roots deep into the soil of life's enduring values
That I may grow toward the stars of my greatest destiny.

Why I Am Still A Priest

Recently a very senior church-person told me that I was probably the worst possible kind of priest — "a populist without loyalty to holy mother church."

We didn't get down to definitions. But if he is a true reflection of "holy mother church", then he's right. To my mind there is an unacceptable face to the human church. And I don't think it's disloyal to say so.

Many years ago, I was asked to speak to a large gathering of priests about how people saw the Catholic Church in Ireland. Another man, now a bishop himself, summed up the resultant discussions accurately:

"There is nothing wrong with the Church," he said, "except that it is run by a bunch of pagans."

That is not the whole truth. But there is enough truth in it to make you want to nod in agreement.

Most priests and bishops in Ireland are good men who are neither paedophiles nor perverts. That needs to be said. Priests working hard in parishes and monasteries, have kept whatever faith there is, alive, often despite the best efforts of "those in charge."

Yet, a disheartening aspect of being a priest today is that no matter how hard one tries, the legacy of resentment resulting from decades of oppressive clericalism in Ireland is so justifiably immense, that few people are without hurt.

And can I let you into a secret? Among those most hurt are the good priests who try harder.

Being a priest was never meant to be easy. And it isn't. It's a strange mixture of sacrifice and compensations. It's a lonely life. Too lonely to be healthy too often.

Do you know what it is like when people expect you to be, at the same time, totally human and totally immune from human weakness?

"The heart has reasons which reason can never understand," Pascal said. Even so it is not easy to rationalise why it is so necessary to reject human love in order to love God "truly."

Patricia Livingston in *Intimacy And Priestly Life* makes this point:

"A priest presides over moments of worship and is sought out in moments of worry. He baptises into new life and anoints as life comes to its close.

"He is called to be an interpreter and a companion on this whole journey, which is a life-time struggle to love.

"If he himself has never really loved, if he has never allowed himself to be vulnerable, it is very difficult for him to lead others on the journey.

"It is almost impossible for him to speak with either compassion or authenticity about what it is like to be human."

It is possible to become so much a 'man for others' that you cease to be a man at all.

You get to a point where you can't recognise love, while attempting to be love in action. And that hurts yourself and those good enough to love you.

After 25 years, there is no doubt in my mind but that priesthood, like so much else in the modern world, is in crisis.

As priests, we're familiar with crises. Usually other people's crises.

We're quick to point out that crisis is a good thing. Far from being an abandoning by God, it's often the only way that God can break into our lives.

The Church would love us to privatise our pain. To say, there must be something wrong with the one in crisis. Because private pain requires only private remedies.

But what happens if troubled lives are a sign that the institution no longer works? Whose crisis is that? For institutions and individuals alike, crises can be resisted but they cannot be avoided. The only way through it is to embrace it.

For centuries priests had no special status. They "should be of impeccable character" and "must not have been married more than once", was Paul's simple instruction in Timothy's letter.

Centuries later, a whole clerical structure was built around the priest. It was practical in its time. A kind of trustworthy civil service which culminated in compulsory celibacy, compensated for by a privileged position in society. Many aspects of that clericalism remain. And very often it is the abuse of clericalism which causes most hurt to the laity.

I've sat with people and listened to their anger and their hurts and marvelled how they had any faith left.

Have you ever imagined how incredibly nauseating it is to hear a family describe how they 'lost' their once innocent son because he was buggered by a priest whom they trusted without question, and who still functions as a priest, while their teenage son is now a drop-out?

How can you find words of comfort for a couple whose marriage is a frigid hell because a Church which preaches love practically forbids them to make love?

How do you justify the slow death of sleeping apart?

Can't you understand the anger that the most precious act given to humans is snatched away by heady arguments and threats of sin and hell and expulsion from Communion?

Try explaining to a couple who have made a go of a second relationship, that the priest who very publicly told them they had no right to come to Mass embarrassing him, is now a 'respected' parish priest. Could you help them find Christ in the human church?

Is there any explanation for the way power is courted, used and sometimes misused in education? The appointment of favoured people as teachers, or an indefensible position with regard to integrated education in the North, are two obvious, and, maybe, not the most serious examples.

Or the off-handed criteria used in determining who is "worthy" and who isn't to receive sacraments?"

This is clericalism that is more concerned with "power" and "control" than with service.

What I'm really saying is that the resentment which is shown to priests now is the backlash to decades of hurt.

I'm not saying all the criticism is justified.

But allowing for the fact that my life is going to be most uncomfortable from now on, I can understand some of the reasons why clerics are pilloried. I can understand the hurt good lay people are experiencing.

If what I say is true, then why do I stay a priest?

You're right to ask the question. It's one which I have wrestled with now for 15 years. I have not sorted it out yet. And I doubt if it should be sorted out. Who said we should be spared confusion? Don't we pray at Mass to be "protected" from all anxiety, not "preserved" from it?

Is there any answer other than that I still believe this is where God wants me to be? That is how He wants me to serve, however uncomfortably. That I must, and want to, give it all I have.

There are days, and they seem to grow with age, when you wonder if you can go on. Yet somehow, the grace comes. The call to strive to bring hope, to be a better human being, maybe even a better priest, is impossible to resist.

And there are "transfiguration" days when it is truly lifegiving being a priest. There are times when I know that, despite all my faults, God uses me to bring peace to a person who is tormented, healing to one ravaged by illness, comfort to a loveless recluse, wholeness to a broken human being, and a glimmer of hope to the despairing.

On Holy Thursday, when every priest renews his vows, he is asked: "Will you unite yourself more closely to Christ and try to become more like Him by joyfully sacrificing your own pleasures and ambition to bring His peace and love to your brothers and sisters?"

That's a hard one to answer, and well nigh impossible to live. But it is what priesthood is all about.

There was an old priest, with whom I lived for many years in the monastery.

I brought him for a meal to celebrate his 89th birthday. He was a lovely, kind, human being.

So I asked him if he had his life as a Passionist priest to live over again, what would he do differently?

"Without hesitation," he said, "I'd be kinder to people who thought they were in sin. I was brought up to believe that a priest who didn't challenge penitents was not being true to his calling.

"I tried to be kind. But I put too many burdens on people already over-burdened."

That's what a really human priest faced a few years before his death. It has haunted me ever since.

We need help from the Church to understand our pain and be lifted up from our over-powering restlessness. We need to experience, like the prodigal son, the power of unconditional love, before we can face challenges.

We need to be told to live and love and risk, because in the end, all will be well.

That's hope. That's why I'm still a priest.

Seeing Is Believing

Henry Ford once asked a young car engineer to name
his chief ambition in life.
The young man said it was to become very rich.
Everything else was secondary.
Sometime later Mr. Ford gave the employee a small
package. When opened, it revealed a pair of metal-rimmed
spectacles, but in place of the lenses was a pair of silver
dollars.
"Put them on," Ford requested. And the young man did.
"Now what do you see?" Ford asked.
"Nothing," the engineer replied,
"the money blocks out everything."
"Maybe your should rethink that ambition of yours,"
said the famous car maker, and walked away.

The Heart Has Its Reasons

Some go to church just for a walk
Some to stare and some to talk
Some go to meet a friend
Some their idle time to spend
Some for general observation
Some for private speculation
Some to seek or find a lover
Some a courtship to discover
Some go there to use their eyes
And newest fashions criticise
Some to show their smart new dress
Some their neighbours to assess
Some to scan a hat or bonnet
Some to price the trimming on it
Some to learn the latest news
That friends at home they may amuse
Some to gossip false and true
Safe hid within the sheltering pew
Some go there to please the squire
Some his daughters to admire
Some the parson go to fawn
Some to lounge and some to yawn
Some because it's thought genteel
Some to vaunt their pious zeal
Some to show how sweet they sing
Some how loud their voices ring
Some the preacher go to hear
His style and voice to praise or jeer
Some forgiveness to implore
Some their sins to varnish o'er
Some to sit and doze and nod
But some to kneel and worship God.

Handling Conflict Positively

I'll be honest. I hate conflict.

I know you're not supposed to admit it these days, when the truly successful person gets his own way, no matter how many other flattened bodies are strewn along the way.

I could never be that "successful."

And yet conflict in our personal lives, in our business dealings, in politics, in religion and certainly in communications is inevitable. One cannot be all things to all people.

So conflict must be handled whether we like it or not. If we can learn to cope with it in a positive way, there can be growth.

Here are a few tips I've picked up.

Keep respect.

Conflict means anger. And where anger is, respect goes out the door. Don't use abusive language. Don't call the other person names. Don't make judgements.

Listen. Interrupt as little as possible. Think before you talk. And remember, just because you're in conflict with somebody doesn't give you permission to hurt or insult deliberately.

Are you always right?

In a dispute each side usually believes they're right and the other wrong. It's hardly ever the case.

Generally speaking, it is one preference against another, one opinion against another. This is always clear if you listen to others row. If we could only get that objectivity into our own disputes.

See the good in the other.

Before you say "but," say "yes". In other words, acknowledge that the other person has a point. It's hard to do it in the heat of battle.

But if you're listening for the truth instead of trying to win, you'll manage. The person you are in conflict with — if they are of goodwill — will probably make sensible points and will appreciate a sign that you hear and agree with some of them.

In some cases your goodness will be rewarded. And if not, it's a sure sign that the other party is not interested in reconciliation.

Talk about feelings and respect feelings.

It's easy to sling accusations. It's much more difficult to explain your own feelings. And more difficult still to respect the other person's feelings.

It's hurtful, demeaning and indefensible to make judgements like "you're a hypocrite."

A person who keeps conflict at that level really wants to hurt, to destroy, the other person. They are certainly not interested in reconciliation nor in the genuine feelings of the other person.

The best principle is to talk about your behaviour versus my feelings, not your motives.

For example, it's much more difficult but much more constructive to say: "I feel hurt, sad, lonely, inadequate, scared, by some of the things you have done to me."

Get beyond the surface.

There are many layers to every person and to every conflict. If you seem to be having World War III over a small issue, then look for the real issues. What is the battle really about? This is what needs to be discussed. There's always a deeper issue.

One row at a time.

This is a practical matter. Most conflicts are a waste of time because too many issues are trotted out and none of them is dealt with.

So have ground rules. Take an issue and discuss it. As soon as one or other wanders away from it, call yourself back to the issue for discussion at this meeting.

One issue at a time is a good discipline so that you can express respect for each other and is a good indication if we're interested in really finding truth peace and harmony.

What's beneath the flying fist?

Anger is not a pleasant emotion to deal with. So talk instead about what's causing your anger and your hurt and your frustration.

Anger is not a primary, but a secondary, emotion. First we get hurt, then we get angry, then we hit back.

Try to find the cause of the hurt, explain the result, frustration and fear, and then let the other side do the same. ،

It's far easier to make an angry attack, sulk and punish the other side with barbs or silence than to say: "I was hurt by what you said and was threatened by what you did."

See if there is a compromise.

Many arguments, conflicts and rows never end because nobody knows what they're looking for. No-one ever proposes a solution.

This is probably because a solution involves compromise, which means settling for less than total annihilation.

But compromise is usually the only resolution possible, unless you're willing to concede completely. Conflict leads to a win/lose situation. Compromise tries to find a win/win situation.

Be generous.

In conflict generosity is essential. Do it for love. Love is the purpose of our lives.

Try to be a person who can recognise issues where you can yield easily and recognise issues where you need to take a stance.

Ask yourself this question.

How many of the issues that we fight over are really worth the struggle?

In the words of the *Our Father,* "Forgive us our sins in the same measure as we forgive those who win against us."

Life is too short to be taken up in conflicts.

Virtue In Action

The Book of Virtues, compiled by William J. Bennett, has been on the bestsellers list in America for years. *The Book of Virtues* is a treasury of moral stories. It has poems, stories and comments highlighting the virtues of responsibility, courage, compassion, loyalty, honesty, friendship, persistence, hard-work, self-discipline and faith. Let me snatch a few samples which give a mere flavour of the book. Of necessity, I cannot use any of the long stories or poems, many of which are brilliant.

* * * * * *

From Aesop's fables comes this little reminder about vanity and self-discipline.

A coal-black crow once stole a piece of meat. She flew to a tree and held the meat in her beak.

A fox, who saw her, wanted the meat for himself, so he looked up the tree and said: "How beautiful you are, my friend. Your feathers are fairer than the dove's. Is your voice as sweet as your form is beautiful? If so, you must be queen of the birds." The crow was so happy in his praise that she opened her mouth to show how she could sing. Down fell the piece of meat. The fox seized upon it and ran away.

Aesop also supplies a simple story about compassion.

One day a great lion lay asleep in the sunshine. A little mouse ran across his paw and wakened him. The great lion was just going to eat him up when the little mouse cried: "Oh please let me go, sir. Some day I may help you."

The lion laughed at the idea that the little mouse could be of any use to him. But he was a good-natured lion, and he set the mouse free.

Not long after, the lion got caught in a net. He tugged and pulled with all his might, but the ropes were too strong. Then he roared loudly. The little mouse heard him, and ran to the spot. He said: "Be still, dear lion, and I will set you free. I will gnaw the ropes."

With his sharp little teeth, the mouse cut the ropes, and the lion came out of the net.

"You laughed at me once," said the mouse. "You thought I was too little to do you a good turn. But see, you owe your life to a poor little mouse."

Which shows that compassion lies within the power of the mighty and the meek.

* * * * * *

Beautiful faces are they that wear
The light of a pleasant spirit there.
Beautiful hands are they that do.
Deeds that are noble, good and true;
Beautiful feet are they that go
Swiftly to lighten another's woe.

* * * * * *

Also there is the famous legend and rhyme based on the demise of King Richard III, whose defeat at Bosworth was immortalised in Shakespeare's line, "A horse, a horse, my kingdom for a horse."

When the King was preparing for battle, he sent a groom to the blacksmith to make sure his horse was ready. The blacksmith told the groom he had no iron to shoe the horse. He'd have to wait. The groom said he couldn't wait and to make do with what he had.

The blacksmith did his best, but he hadn't enough iron to make nails to fasten the fourth shoe.

The groom told him to make do.

In battle, Richard was galloping to help his men when his horse's shoe fell off. The horse stumbled and rolled over. Richard was thrown to the ground. His men deserted him when they saw his distress. Richard was captured and Henry won the battle. And since that time people have said:

For want of a nail, a shoe was lost.
For want of a shoe, a horse was lost.
For want of a horse, a battle was lost,
For want of a battle a kingdom was lost,
And all for the want of a horse-shoe nail.

* * * * * *

In the section on Friendship I found an African folk -tale.

A little frog and a little snake met as strangers in the bush one day, and played together all day.

"Watch what I can do," said frog-child, and he hopped high into the air. "I'll teach you if you want," he offered.

So he taught snake-child how to hop, and together they hopped up and down the path through the bush.

"Now watch what I can do," said snake-child, and he crawled on his belly straight up the trunk of a tall tree. "I'll teach you if you want."

So he taught frog-child how to slide on his belly and climb trees.

After a while they both grew hungry and decided to go home for lunch, but they promised each other to meet again next day.

"Thanks for teaching me how to hop," called snake-child.

"Thanks for teaching me how to crawl up trees," called frog-child.

Then they each went home.

"Look what I can do, mother," cried frog-child, crawling on his belly.

"Where did you learn how to do that?" his mother asked.

"Snake-child taught me," he answered. "We played together in the bush this morning, He's my new friend."

"Don't you know that the snake family is a bad family?" his mother asked. "They have poison in their teeth. Don't ever let me see you crawling on your belly either. It isn't proper."

Meanwhile snake-child went home and hopped up and down for his mother to see.

"Who taught you to do that?" she asked.

"Frog-child did," he said, "He's my new friend."

"What foolishness," said his mother. "Don't you know that we've been on bad terms with the frog family for longer than we can remember. The next time you play with frog-child, catch him and eat him up. And stop that hopping. It isn't our custom."

So next morning when frog-child met snake-child in the bush, he kept his distance.

"I'm afraid I can't go crawling with you today," he called, hopping back a hop or two.

Snake-child eyed him quietly, remembering what his mother had told him. "If he gets too close, I'll spring at him and eat him," he thought. But then he remembered how much fun they had had together, and how nice frog-child had been to teach him how to hop. So he sighed sadly to himself and slid away into the bush.

And from that day onward, frog-child and snake-child never played together again. But they often sat alone in the sun, each thinking about their one day of friendship.

* * * * * *

Perhaps my favourite story of all is Leo Tolstoy's Russian tale, which I'll paraphrase for you until you're lucky enough to read it in full.

In a little Russian town there lived a cobbler, Martin.

He lived in a tiny basement with one window, which looked onto the street.

From the window, he could see only feet. But that was all he needed to see. He recognised people by their shoes, since he had made most of them.

He was always a good man, and in old age when his wife died, he spent long winter nights reading his Bible by candlelight.

One night he read about a man who invited Jesus into his house and didn't even offer water to wash his feet. Yet a sinful woman, an outcast, anointed His feet.

Martin thought long and hard and wondered how he would welcome Jesus, should he ever come to visit him. Martin concluded he probably would be like the man and wouldn't welcome Jesus in the proper way at all.

He drifted off to sleep. While he slept, he thought he heard a voice telling him: "Martin, look in the street tomorrow. I will come to visit you."

Martin was excited. Could it be that Jesus was really coming to visit? He looked intently on everyone near his shop.

First came an old soldier. He was poor and lived on charity. Today he had a shovel and began clearing away the snow. The work was too hard for him and he nearly collapsed.

Martin brought him in and gave him hot tea. Martin explained he was waiting for Jesus. But the old soldier thanked him and told Martin that he couldn't read and he knew very little about Jesus.

After he left, Martin saw a young woman with flimsy clothes carrying a baby in her arms. She and the baby were shivering and cold, and close to collapse.

Martin went upstairs and brought her in from the cold. She was frightened by the old man with the spectacles on his nose.

She explained she had no milk for the baby as she had not eaten herself.

She had pawned her clothes earlier.

Martin gave her soup and bread and went upstairs and gave her the clothes in the wardrobe, which had never been used since his wife died.

The woman was delighted. She crossed herself and said: "God bless you."

The day passed and Martin did not see Jesus.

In the evening, an old woman came selling apples. She carried a bundle of sticks on her back. It was heavy and she was tired. So she laid it on the ground.

As she did, a young boy came racing past and quickly stole an apple.

She was furious and grabbed him and tongue-lashed him and beat him.

Martin went to the street and separated them.

He told the old woman he would pay for the apple. He convinced the boy to ask for forgiveness, to apologise and promise not to do it again.

He advised the old woman to forgive, because older people should be wiser and must lead by example.

She thought about her own seven sons and the trouble they had got into and calmed down. She patted the boy on the head and let him go.

She was about to pick up the sticks, but before she could, the boy did it for her. "Let me carry them, Granny," he said.

And off they went together, chatting as they went. And the old woman forgot to take the money for the apple.

When Martin closed his shop that night, he was very disappointed. Jesus had not come.

Sadly, by candlelight, he took his Bible down to read it. But before he did, he nodded off to sleep.

As he woke he heard footsteps. He turned around and there he saw a group behind him.

"It is I," said the soldier.

"It is I," said the woman with the child.

"It is I," said the old woman and the young boy together.

Martin grew peaceful. He put on his spectacles and read the Bible at the open page in front of him.

"I was hungry and you gave me to eat, thirsty and you gave me to drink...as long as you did it to one of these my brethren, you did it to me..." was what he read.

Martin knew he wasn't imagining. He knew his dream had come true. Jesus had visited him. And Martin had indeed welcomed him.

(The Book of Virtues, an anthology compiled by William J Bennett, is published by Simon and Schuster. My thanks to David Hall of Enniskillen who went to extraordinary lengths to get the book for me.)

Bald-headed

Some people, who are rather bald, have long been used to getting comfort from the remark that "Grass doesn't grow on a busy street." These days, however, the comfort fast disappears, when somebody is certain to respond: "There's no sense in putting a roof on an empty barn." But perhaps the nicest one of all comes from a preacher who is bald. He was shy about his baldness and made self- conscious remarks about it during his sermons.

Then one old lady pointed out to him that he shouldn't be ashamed of his baldness. She said: "God makes all heads beautiful, but some are so beautiful that He had no need to cover them with hair."

Could Married Deacons Help Save The Church?

There are all kinds of priests and parishes in Africa, just as there are here. Some thriving and some dead.

But they.are getting vocations to the priesthood and religious life there. And they are trying to empower lay people — much more enthusiastically than we are here.

Maybe it's because people there are less cynical, and priests are less attached to power or permanence.

For example, in two of the parishes I spent time in, they had permanent married deacons.

They were married men who had spent more than five years, part-time, being trained for leading people in prayer as well as preaching.

The system worked brilliantly. In big parishes with one priest, it is not possible for the priest to do everything. Choices have to be made.

These married deacons baptised children and adults, buried the dead, married young loving couples, preached at Masses, visited the sick, trained Eucharistic ministers, and held Communion Services for the whole parish when Mass was not available.

They took over the parish if the priest needed to be elsewhere.

Remember: they were laymen, married, holding down jobs and working voluntarily for the Church.

I depended on them for advice as well as help.

What amazed me was how the people accepted a fellow parishioner "doing" their weddings, baptisms and family funerals.

They accepted the fact that there was really no need to have Mass offered to make these occasions holy.

There are more than 12,000 such deacons throughout the world, yet as far as I know there is not a single married deacon in Ireland.

So how can we say we have a shortage of priests?

How is it that we priests are so tied up in administration that we don't have time to visit parishioners?

What does it say about the structure of the Church here that we labour under impossible work-loads and still won't budge on the principle that the priest must have sole control of everything in the parish, from schools to churches to football clubs?

What does it say about the possibility of married priests? The community there accepted totally a married man from their community, doing everything a priest does, except offering Mass and ministering Reconciliation.

It works so well that shortly one religious order in black townships will be putting their priests into parishes on three-year contracts.

During those three years, they will train the laity to run a priestless parish on their own. The priests will then move on and train another group in another parish.

Why is it that in Northern Ireland we say we have not enough priests even to visit inter-denominational schools? Does anyone believe that?

Is it not time for a radical rethink on the kind and shape of Church we take for granted here?

Won't lay people and priests simply have to get used to new images of Church?

Won't lay people have to accept more responsibility and won't bishops and priests have to let go of some power?

During my time in South Africa I met great priests who had learned to let go, to trust people. And I met committed lay people who ran parishes brilliantly.

For example, I never handled a collection in any of the seven churches I dealt with.

Lay people took up the collection, counted it, banked it and a finance committee decided how it should be spent. The chairperson of the committee was the person who addressed the congregation about money-matters, not the priest.

I'm not saying it was a perfect system, but I was struck by the trust and the commitment involved.

Trust is a big issue in Ireland now. I'm often asked now if people will ever trust any priest again?

Equally, I could ask if we priests will ever learn to trust lay-people where it really matters — with power and money.

I've said often that, in my opinion, the biggest problem facing the Catholic church is not married priests or women priests — important as those two issues are — but how we can de-clericalise the Church.

Who, for example, even thinks of asking the people of the parish what kind of priest they would need in their parish? When was the last time you were consulted about your new parish priest?

Has anyone asked why parish priests have to be appointed for life rather than for a fixed term?

As a priest I have occasionally been consulted about the appointment of Bishops. In all honesty though, most priests are fiercely angry at how Bishops are imposed on them with the minimum of consultation and with absolutely no real input into the eventual choice. There is a charade of consultation.

The appointments are often already made before the consultation takes place.

Clandestine organisations in effect have a big say in the crucial appointments.

There will be no trust, no new beginning, without radical changes in the Church.

Dwindling vocations are God's way of bringing us to our senses. Secretive appointments, covering up unworthy candidates, power-hungry clerics and an hierarchical Church which treated its people with something akin to disdain have got us into this mess.

Who talks seriously about "the good old days" now?

Papering over the cracks and hoping things will "return to normal" won't work. People are too hurt, too disillusioned.

Priests who have given the best years of their lives to the Church rightly feel let down. Only faith in God keeps them going. But even their faith is close to breaking point now.

Good priests and forgiving lay-people have kept the Church alive. And now they feel they have been misled, misguided and mistaken.

We must be prepared to change radically, to dismantle an oppressive male monolith which passes for the institutional Church.

But it is not a matter of keeping quiet and hoping that the storm will pass.

It won't.

The Cross In My Pocket

A walker cheated death when a thunderbolt carrying millions of volts struck a gold crucifix round his neck.

The lightning blew him off his feet, ripped half his clothes away and branded the outline of a cross on his skin.

The walker said that his wife had bought him the cross when their little boy was born. Only for it, he thought he would have been killed. He intends to wear it for the rest of his life, for luck.

That was how the papers reported the walker's miracle escape. But perhaps the Cross is something more than just a sign of luck. My own views are well summed up in *The Cross In My Pocket*.

I carry a cross in my pocket,
A simple reminder to me
Of the fact that I am a Christian
No matter where I may be.

This little cross is not magic
Nor is it a good luck charm
It isn't meant to protect me
From every physical harm.

It's not for identification
For all the world to see
It's simple an understanding
Between my Saviour and me.

When I put my hand in my pocket
To bring out a coin or a key
The cross is there to remind
Of the price he paid for me.

It reminds me, too, to be thankful
For His blessings day by day
And to strive to serve Him better
In all that I do and say.

It's also a daily reminder,
Of the peace and comfort I share,
With all who know my Master
And give themselves to His care.

So, I carry a cross in my pocket,
Reminding no one but me
That Jesus Christ is the Lord of my life
If only I'll let Him be.

"Mummy, I Think I'm Pregnant."

Let's talk about sex outside marriage.

At regular intervals now, the media get a rush of morality to the head. For the rest of the year they are quite content to condemn anybody who would even hint that sexual moral standards should be maintained.

Then somebody in authority — a bishop, prince or politician — steps out of line and the latent pulpit thumpers raise the dust.

My story today may be small fry to you, but stay with me as I share part of the life and rather sad times of Mandy Murphy (not her real name).

One morning, getting ready for school, she became violently ill. Her mother found her bent over in the bathroom.

A bad flu was suggested.

"It's not a flu," said Mandy. "I think I'm pregnant."

Just like that.

Mandy was 17.

The images of a child disappeared in a minute.

Mandy says the shocked look on her mother's face is something she will never forget.

She was put to bed and when her mother got herself a hot cup of tea, she sat down and heard the story.

Mandy and her boyfriend went, as part of a group, on a weekend camping. One night they all sat around and drank beer. The rest of the night was a bit blurred, but Mandy says that night was the only time she made love to anyone.

It's a night she hardly remembers but will never forget.

Years of experience have taught me that when a teenage girl becomes pregnant the whole family becomes pregnant.

At 17 Mandy was the eldest daughter. They thought it would never happen.

In olden days, and too frequently even today, the first thought would have been for marriage.

The Murphys did think it could be the best solution. But looking back it proves they were acting out of shock that they even considered marriage.

Abortion was out of the question.

So they wanted to find out how they could help Mandy.

Since the young man had been going out with Mandy for about three months, she phoned him. Like her, he was in his last year at school. They met in a cafe.

Mandy was hurt by his reaction. His first question was:

"Are you sure it's me?"

A week later he phoned to say he was sorry. He, too, was reacting in shock.

The two families met and it was important they should.

Again marriage was ruled out but it was a frosty meeting.

The boy's father, a professional man, talked about a "medical solution". The Murphys think he was talking about an abortion. But from there on it was a revolving door conversation. The same lines came out again and again and no progress was made.

The two families, even though they lived in the same parish, have kept out of each other's way since.

Mandy dropped out of school, the boy went on and did his Leaving Cert and will probably go to college.

The teachers felt that Mandy could come to school if she wished and some of them offered to give her private tuition at home. Unfortunately, because she was sick so long, it wouldn't have worked.

The next problem was what to do when the baby was born. Would Mandy give up the baby for adoption?

If she didn't who would rear the child?

Would the grandparents?

What would happen if Mandy married later and wanted to take the baby with her?

What about the other children in the family?

Mandy has had her baby.

She wanted to keep her baby and the moment she cuddled her little boy for the first time she knew she could never give him up.

Her family are a good support. Her mother looks after the baby as much as she can and they hope, come September, Mandy will go back to school.

There are problems. She's had to grow up much too quickly. Her mother notices that she's still a child herself. Yet she's a mother too.

These days many young people believe the media hype that sex before marriage is the "done thing." Perhaps it is. But even if it is, it's just as well to know what the consequences are.

There is much talk about protection against AIDS. And rightly so. But there are other dangers associated with casual sex.

Young people look for love and closeness. The new style of family means they often don't get it at home.

In the arms of a boyfriend/girlfriend they find that love and closeness, that feeling of being wanted, they crave for.

And often they're not able to cope with the emotional turmoil. And who could blame them?

It is not always promiscuity which forces young people into tempestuous situations.

The way we live today doesn't help. Young people find no difficulty being together alone for long periods. Often parents leave them at home and go away for weekends or holidays. How they expect their children to cope is beyond me.

But parents always think that nothing could happen their children. They have a hopeless knowledge of human nature. They think their children are protected with a special innocence.

Alcohol is another major reason for pregnancies outside marriage.

Parents will settle for their children drinking. These days it's better than going on drugs. It's the lesser of two evils.

Again, they forget that alcohol is a drug too and that drinking among teenagers who can't cope with life, even when they are sober, is a recipe for disaster.

If you remember, Mandy hardly remembers the night which changed her life dramatically.

Sometimes, I wish parents spent as much time worrying about their children at weekends and at parties as they do about what school they attend, how many points they will achieve, or what job they'll get after school.

I wish parents would discuss sexual behaviour with their children. It's not a matter of having a hang-up about sex. Parents and schools could do much more to highlight the dangers and the foolishness of casual and cheap sex outside of marriage.

Or is it that parents themselves don't believe it's wrong?

Could it be their own lifestyle that's under the microscope?

Parents need to have convictions and to be firm in them.

And teenagers need parents with solid convictions. They need parents with standards.

The media and society are the influences which will give children their "standards" if parents opt out with the silent approach. Silence is not golden.

In short, teenagers need to be told about the consequences of casual sex. There is a high price to be paid.

These days we know that abusive sex leaves a scar on the person which is almost impossible to heal.

We also pretend that casual sex is harmless as long as it is with consent and with contraception — it's okay if you separate real love from what happens "between the sheets."

Wrong.

Casual sex always trivialises love and ultimately the person themselves. Sex always touches something very deep, whether we know it or not, and can leave a terrible hurt if people are "used," just because of a "horny" feeling, to use the awful language of the alleyway.

That's about as plain as I can put it!

A very old Chinese proverb

If there be righteousness in the heart, there will be beauty in the character. If there is beauty in the character there will be harmony in the home. If there is harmony in the home, there will be order in the nation.
When there is order in each nation, there will be peace in the world.

Exams Can Kill!

"My son hung himself last year, just before the last day of his exams," said the frail woman sitting opposite me, with a shocking frankness.

She was on holidays, visiting some friends and wanted to talk. Not only that, she wanted me to say an encouraging word to those doing exams this year. The kind of encouraging word she wished she had said to her son.

There's no doubt about it, exam pressure is one, among many, of the complex reasons why young people take their lives.

But even worse, the desire to do well is so much a part of modern culture, modern families and the education system, that hundreds of young people totter on the edge.

Not because they are bad. Not because they are stupid.

Not even because they haven't worked. But the realisation that even their best may still leave them "failures."

I was never much good at exams myself. I worked like a demon. I studied into the small hours of the night. But I had no confidence in my own ability.

I am, by nature, hyper-nervous. I scraped through exams which I should have excelled in. I never did myself justice.

And when I had done my last exam I can honestly say I began to live for the first time. I was 24 years old and already six months a priest.

And if I never have to do an exam again, I'll be happy.

So, let me say this. I've managed reasonably well in life since then. Exam results would be a deplorably weak criterion to judge any person. To do badly in an exam, even to fail it, does not make you a failure as a person.

I'm not going to tell you how to do an exam. *I'm telling you that no matter how you do in an exam, you are still a valuable, lovable, talented person with the possibility of greatness.*

Look at yourself in the mirror and repeat that sentence three times.

Self esteem is vital in life. You must believe that you are a good person doing the best you know how.

Yes, you will make mistakes. And you will fail at different projects.

And you will fail at relationships. You'll be broken-hearted and devastated. Deep down though, realise that you can learn from your errors and discover good points.

Self-esteem does not mean you are arrogant or self-centered.

It doesn't mean you think you are the best-looking, best-dressed, most talented person around. It doesn't mean you think you are better than anybody else.

Self-esteem begins with the realisation that, when God said, "Love your neighbour as yourself," He meant that you should first of all love yourself.

Look at yourself honestly and answer these questions:

Is life fairly good or pretty rotten for you?

The way you see the world is a good indicator as to how you see yourself. Usually people who see good in themselves will see good in the world. And usually people who always criticise the world around them have a pretty dim view of themselves.

How do you talk about other people?

If mostly your conversation is putting others down, knocking everything, complaining and accusing, then you say much more about yourself than you do about others.

Are there things in your life that you hide from everybody else? Maybe even from yourself?

That can tell you two things. There's a shadow side to yourself that you haven't yet made friends with. You need to accept that there is good and bad in you. That both are valuable, and that both need to be examined and worked on daily. If you are afraid to look at your own life, then you haven't given yourself a chance to be fully human or fully alive.

So, before you do any exams, sit quietly with a blank sheet of paper in front of you and write down your five strongest points. You won't be asked any of these in an examination. But if you've got them right, your exam paper will be worth reading.

Half our trouble in examinations is that we try to impress others. If we are confident and comfortable with ourselves we don't need to impress anybody. We impart our information neither in an arrogant nor self-effacing way.

The biggest enemy is fear. Fear is not something to be ashamed of. It can be the biggest enemy you have or it can be your greatest asset.

Recognising that you are fearful, but refusing to be paralysed by it, is an important lesson to learn. Don't surrender to fear, but use it to motivate yourself. And once you learn to make it work for you, fear will become your best friend. Confront your fears and then conquer them.

That's courage. It helps you to be honest with yourself and make good choices.

Learn to like yourself. Be your best self. Take stock of yourself. Write down your gifts, your strengths and your failings.

Make plans. Decide what's important, decide what you can do, and then do it. Develop the skills you need. Practical skills.

But most of all, be realistic. It's good to be daring but don't try the impossible.

Say "no" to negative thinking. Forgive yourself. Allow yourself to make mistakes without concluding that you are a failure.

Find support in your friends and then support them.

If you are a parent, there are some things you can do too. First of all, don't exert too much pressure.

The lady who came to me from England, after her son had committed suicide, had at least that consolation. She knew she hadn't put pressure on her son.

But until the day she goes to her grave, she will feel guilty because she didn't encourage him. She had seen him make exams the only test of success or failure in his life. No exam is that important.

At The Heart Of Family Life

In his book, *Decline and Fall Of The Roman Empire,* Edward Gibbon proposed five reasons why that civilisation collapsed.

1. The undermining of the dignity of the home. The basic cell of human society.
2. Ever-increasing taxes.
3. The mad craze for pleasure, with sports and plays becoming more exciting, more brutal and more immoral.
4. The building of great armaments when the real enemy was within.
5. The decay of religion, whose leaders lost touch with life and lost their credibility to guide.

Gibbon wrote that 200 years ago. Does it apply to family life today?

It is a simple fact that no family was/is perfect. Family, like marriage, like life, is a process, not an arrival point.

The amazing thing is not the number of marriages and families that fail, but the number that survive and prosper.

Through the years, there have been many family-wreckers. Booze, interfering relatives, poverty, joblessness.

Re-establishing family values for the modern society is vital, therefore.

New family values will have to give an equal voice to women.

They will be based on sexual openness (not permissiveness). Children being born now, bombarded as they are with every detail about sex, will at least be spared some of the old hypocrisies.

Family values will highlight love and commitment as a necessary part of sexual conduct. How to have permanent commitment in a changing society is one of the great challenges today.

Family values will have to discover ways to be holy in secular surroundings.

No so long ago, couples who got married could be reasonably certain of staying together for life.

Such assumed stability is not part of modern society.

Many young people getting married now, come from dysfunctional families. Therefore, they will have different expectations and different models.

A failed relationship is not necessarily a failed life.

If your marriage hasn't worked out the way you hoped it would, don't feel a failure.

If you are a child of a marriage that has broken up, or if you are caught between two parents pulling you apart, there ought to be encouragement for you in the family we call Church.

No matter what your position in life is, single or married, a success or a failure, God never says you are outside His help, His care, His understanding or His compassion.

If your marriage has been a success, thank God for it. Don't feel guilty: you probably worked hard at it. Celebrate it. But you are lucky and once you accept it as a blessing you'll be slow to judge somebody who wasn't so blessed.

A good family is a place where you learn to share, to care and be fair. It's a place where there is good communication and the secret of good communication is to take the secrets out of it.

They say that a typical Irish husband is a man who hasn't kissed his wife for 20 years but will thump the first man who tries to. That's too near the truth to be funny.

Communication is difficult today. But unless you make time for each other, it's impossible to get to know each other. And it must be prime time too.

Communication within a family means that we accept our differences.

It is essential to know that nobody can make you happy. And nobody can make you unhappy.

If your husband is a workaholic, then you must confront him and challenge him.

Because he's wasting his life, is no excuse for you wasting yours.

More than ever, couples go into marriage as equals now.

If you think you can still be a domineering male, following your grandfather's model, you haven't a hope.

Equally so, women should not be afraid of their own femininity, despite modern society's blatant attempt to suppress those beautiful qualities.

Each member of the family, not just husband and wife, should be free to share feelings. And they should be free, if necessary, to be "failures."

Is your family open enough, for example, to accept a child who is a homosexual?

If your daughter became pregnant, would she rather have an abortion than tell you?

If your child was unhappy, would you read the signs?

Would your child be one who would take his own life, rather than admit to failure?

Those are stark questions for any parent to answer. They are questions for each member of the family to be free to answer honestly.

Give children reasonable guide-lines. Talk to your spouse so that both of you are saying the same thing. There's enough confusion around, without each parent giving a different message.

Simply because a child turns out, in your eyes, a failure, doesn't mean that you as a parent are a failure. Don't take it as a personal tragedy everytime your child makes a mistake.

Recently, I was working with a group of young people. As an exercise I asked them to tell their parents how they would like to be treated. These are some of the points they made:

Treat all children with equal affection.

Develop a comradeship between grown-ups and children.

Always answer questions, allow discussions, allow differences of opinion.

Don't blame, punish or put down your children in the presence of outsiders.

Concentrate on some good points, don't always harp on the failings.

It's all summed up in *Children Learn What They Live*.

If a child lives with criticism, they learn to condemn.

If a child lives with hostility, they learn to fight.

If a child lives with ridicule, they learn to be shy.

If a child lives with shame, they learn to feel guilty.

If a child lives with tolerance, they learn to be patient.

If a child lives with encouragement, they learn confidence.
If a child lives with praise, they learn to appreciate.
If a child lives with fairness, they learn justice.
If a child lives with security, they learn to have faith.
If a child lives with approval, they learn to like themselves.
If a child lives with acceptance and friendship, they learn to
find love in the world.

Don't Judge Others Too Harshly

Pray do not find fault with the man who limps,
or stumbles along the road,
Unless you have worn the shoes he wears,
or struggled beneath his load.
There may be tacks in his shoes that hurt,
though hidden away from view.
The burden he bears, placed on your back,
might cause you to stumble, too.
Don't sneer at the man who's down today,
unless you have felt the blow,
That caused his fall, or felt the shame
that only the fallen know.
You may be strong, but still the blows that were his,
if dealt to you,
In the self-same way at the self-same time,
might cause you to stagger, too.
Don't be harsh with the man who sins,
or pelt him with word and stone,
Unless you are sure, yea doubly sure,
that you have no sins of your own.
For, you know, perhaps, if the tempter's voice
should whisper soft to you,
As it did to him when he went astray,
'twould cause you to falter, too!

(Author Unknown)

Priests And Sexual Abuse

In the old days if you suggested a priest would sexually abuse children, you'd be laughed out of town in some places.

And yet, we all knew teachers — priests, brothers and laymen — with a "reputation". You stayed well clear of them.

Yet, the first families to make charges against priests were met by denials, cover-ups and sometimes downright aggression.

Over the last few years the sexual abuse of children in general has been "outed". Incest was a taboo subject, even when I first wrote about it 15 years ago.

Now the focus is on sexual abuse by members of the clergy. There are hundreds of known cases throughout the world, and a growing number here in Ireland.

It is admitted even by the Pope. In a talk to the Bishops in the U.S. he said: "I fully share your sorrow and your concern, especially your concern for the victims so seriously hurt by these misdeeds."

Father Andrew Greely, never one to understate a case, has said that it's the worst problem to face the church since the Reformation.

In Chicago, one of the leading dioceses to deal with sexual abuse by their clergy in a proper way, Cardinal Bernadin spends over 30 per cent of his time dealing with cases of child sexual abuse by his priests.

And Cardinal O' Connor of New York admits: "It's getting increasingly difficult for some priests and some Bishops to hold their heads up: everyone is under suspicion".

So, how widespread is it? Experts differ. What is certain is that between three and six per cent of all priests are sexual abusers.

That's a considerable number. There are 40, 000 priests in the United States. So, somewhere between 1, 500 and 3, 000 priests sexually abuse children.

And when you consider that each abuser is believed to abuse an average of 10 victims, you can see how many victims are suffering greatly.

There are some interesting comparisons between sexual abuse in society and sexual abuse by members of the clergy.

Girls are the victims in most cases of child sexual abuse in the general population, whilst boys are more likely to be the victims of priests.

Little is known about child sexual abuse in general. We are only now recognising that it is widespread among the general population and often among parents themselves.

It is not confined to members of the Catholic Church either. There's a growing file against members of the clergy of other denominations as well.

Some say that there is a higher incidence of sexual abuse in clergy (in all denominations) because sexual predators enter the ministry so that they can be in touch with vulnerable people.

People who are sexual abusers of children are people who violate trust. Clergy are people who are predominately in a position of trust. That's an added attraction for potential abusers.

There is no denying that abuse by a priest is the worst form of abuse because so many people believe that priests represent God. Abused victims are generally those who are the most trusting and most religious in the community.

The cause of so much abuse is not easy to pinpoint. Some experts are beginning to believe that abusers have damage to the part of the brain which controls conscience and inhibition.

There are two basic types of abusers. One type is the *regressed.*

These are people who grew up psychosexually and socially quite well, but in time of emotional stress slip back to feelings and behaviour which are focused to their adolescence and childhood.

This is often the case with incest within families too.

Priests who fall in times of regression are those who face increased stress due to overwork, loneliness, pastoral failure, clashes with authority figures such as their bishop, or rejection by parishioners.

There is a lot of stress in the lives of priests today. Hence the high incidence.

The second type is *fixated* or *arrested* i.e. people who grew up physically but not psychosexually and socially. They are sexually attracted only to children or young adolescents because they themselves are psychosexually still at the childhood or teenage stage.

Worst of all with priests is the way it is often rationalised in their life. Instead of thinking about it in moral terms, they delude themselves into thinking that the boy or girl has been deprived of attention and affection and needs their tenderness.

Others will say that they are acting on behalf of God and that the child is bad and needs to be punished.

Still others are so deluded by their own importance that they think they have power over people at every level of their being.

"Power mania" is the biggest sickness amongst clergy today. Abuse is only one manifestation of it.

Strangely enough, celibacy seems to have little to do with the high incidence of child sexual abuse. Though, if abusers were in a normal family set-up, in times of stress they would be redirected in their outlets.

Almost all agree that the illness is well in place long before priests make their commitment to celibacy.

That is why there is an urgent need to reform training in seminaries.

For example, if a seminarian or a young priest prefers to work almost exclusively with young people, that should act as a red flag.

It's all right to work with children and young people part of the time, but a balanced pastor has to relate to adults. If he can't, he has a serious problem.

In America, where so far over 400 million dollars has been paid out by dioceses in compensation, the president of the Bishops Conference said recently: "Few in society and church understood the problem well in the past. People tended to treat sexual abuse as they did alcoholism — as a moral fault for which repentance and a change of scene would result in a change of behaviour.

"Far more aggressive steps are needed to protect the innocent, treat the perpetrator and safeguard our children."

A legitimate criticism of the Church so far is that they have been more concerned about protecting priests than about helping the victims.

This is changing.

Almost all dioceses and religious orders are in the process of drawing up a policy.

Some common points are:

•   A prompt investigation of allegations of abuse.

- A prompt suspension of the priest or religious and a referral for evaluation and treatment if the investigation supports the charges.
- Co-operation with civil authorities if the victim files criminal charges.
- Help and support for victims.
- Openness with the community.
- Better screening and training for seminarians.

False accusations are a worrying new development. In many cases, accusations are made against individual clergy which have to be investigated but are difficult to sustain. These are hardest for those in authority.

Another big problem is what to do with a clerical offender. Can he return to the ministry?

Some therapists believe that offenders can return to work if they don't deal with children. But this worries victims because the priesthood is not a right and no risk is acceptable.

Some points are clear:
- Some abusive priests are clearly predators who deserve to spend a long time in prison.
- Others are weak, sick people who have, on another level, many talents and gifts and could become useful members of society.
- Either way, a Church which ordains men has an obligation to society to help them and protect society from them.
- Because of the special bond of trust that priests have, there is a special obligation to ensure that that trust is never broken.

(The research for this article has been mainly in American publications, *U.S. Catholic, Sunday Visitor, The Chicago Tribune, U.S.A. Today and Time Magazine*. Books worth reading: *Is Nothing Sacred?* by Reverend Marie Fortune, and *Lead Us Not Into Temptation* by Jason Berry.)

I'm Dancing As Fast As I Can

God grant me the serenity to accept things I cannot change, the courage to change the things I can and the wisdom to know the difference.

This is one of my favourite prayers in life. It is a prayer that comes from the Alcoholics Anonymous programme. It is a good prayer because it has three essential strands of prayer and healthy attitudes.

The first is *acceptance*. Probably the hardest thing in life is to accept the situation we are in. We always want to change it — to move somewhere else — to think that we could be better in a different place. It is a help to ask God to accept the situation you are in, because that's the best place to start. It is the only real world.

The second is a request for *courage*, most important. There is an old proverb which says that we should "work as if everything depended on us and pray as if everything depended on God".

And, of course, the third is the *wisdom* to deal with the problem anyway. The basis of the prayer though, is that we should recognise serenity should it happen to us.

In the hurly burly of life, I must admit, I am not sure I would recognise serenity. There are some days when I think I have found it. Usually those days begin when I have time to put the day in perspective — to pray.

As St. Francis of Assisi said, "Every morning you should prepare your soul for a tranquil day," and, very definitely, a prayer at the beginning of the day, is one sure way of putting tranquillity into the day.

I have also discovered that on the days when you feel saddest, it is a help if you can act happy. It is not a question of acting out life or of trying to be two-faced about things. It is really trying to see the bright side of things, not to let the sadness and depression take over the whole day. Even on the worst days, good things happen.

There is an autobiography called *I Am Dancing As Fast As I Can*. It was written by the head of the C.B.S. Film Company in America, a lady who suffered severe depression.

She took the title from a line in a play. The play was about a couple going away on a weekend to try to get their marriage together again.

They wanted to enjoy everything to the full. The husband was urging his wife to enjoy it even more. The highs were never high enough. While they were out on the dance floor he wanted more zest! Her answer was: "I am dancing as fast as I can." It is a lovely title.

The lady took it as the story of her life too. Sometimes she was pressurised to enjoy life in a way that she couldn't. She got peace only when she was able to say "No" to certain aspects of life. She was dancing as fast as she could. She didn't have to fit into someone else's identikit.

When she was in the depths of depression, she went to a psychologist. She said she could see nothing good in her life. All she wanted to do was commit suicide.

The psychologist advised her: "Please take one huge deep breath." Which she did. And then she breathed out. She did this several times before the psychologist eventually said: "There's something good. You are breathing."

That's what I mean by trying to see the bright side of life on occasions.

• There is no day that's so bad that you are not breathing. It is important not to let the whole world know how sad you are. Save sadness for your very personal friends. I have also found it a help not to worry about useless problems. I'm not saying you shouldn't worry at all because that would be abnormal. But I am just as convinced that we worry far too much about useless problems.

Have a look at the really important things and you will find enough worries in them. The unimportant things are not worth worrying about, simply because they are unimportant.

It was, I think, St. Augustine who said that we should trust the past entirely to the mercy of God, the present to His tender love, and the future to His providence.

Another thing: It is important to do what you are doing.

The day I have most problems is when I start doing several

things at the same time. I usually end up being totally frustrated. Nothing ever gets done. Whatever job you are doing, that is the one you should do. Take the next one in its turn. One task at a time is quite enough.

Of the people who come to me, I find that most of them believe their lives are in the control of others. We all do it. Other people hurt us. Other people make us feel inferior. Other people upset our day.

- There are very few days in which we upset our own day and yet it is a very simple rule of life — that nobody can upset you without your consent.

- Nobody can make you feel inferior unless you allow them to make you feel inferior. So don't. You have control of your life. It is not selfish. It is quite simply you taking control of your life and making a decision that some people are not going to upset you, because they have no right to steal your peace.

- If the same people keep upsetting you day after day, then the fault really is your own, unless the one who hurts you is the one you love. Then a different set of values take over.

- A sense of humour is one of the best gifts we have from God. All of us have a sense of humour of some kind. But we don't always develop it. A good loud belly-laugh is one of the greatest cures for the blues I know.

- Never lose a sense of proportion — which means don't take yourself too seriously. Pope John XXIII, when he was elected Pope, spent some nights worrying about the awful responsibility that had been put upon him. One night God said, "John, take your sleep. The problems will be there in the morning and I'll take charge of them for you during the night." After that John never took himself too seriously. And slept soundly.

- Probably the best bit of advice of all is the simplest - take time to relax: take time to enjoy yourself. I can hear those who really know me laugh out loud at that.

- The Scriptures are full of advice to us and it can all be summed up in that one phrase — enjoy the present moment.

To put it in perspective, remember that wonderful quote from the Talmud: "Man (or woman) will have to answer to God for all the legitimate pleasures which he failed to enjoy."

The Night My Brutal Husband Took A Life

There are times when I wonder about human nature. I think I have heard it all. Then I hear the sad story of another's suffering. And I come near to despair. You'll read this letter and think: "He's making it up." But I'm not. This is exactly as the lady wrote it:

"It was the end of the day. I was tired after a long day's work," *she began her story of horror.*

The children and myself had supper. They were washed and ready for bed. I wasn't sure if my husband would come back that night as he often stayed away overnight. But I had to wait. The children were getting tired. I wanted to keep them up a little longer as I was scared but didn't want to let them know. I joined in with them as they played with their toys. They asked now and then if Dad would be long more or would he be drunk. I tried to be cheerful and talked to them about whatever topic they mentioned. I knew when it was late he surely had a bad day with the horses or had an argument with someone.

The car came fast with a sudden jam of brakes. He revved the engine for a further few minutes. Then he stormed in saying, "Everything alright in this house?" When the dog recovered he crawled under the stove which had legs on it. The children ran to the hallway in fear. My daughter wet herself and they were both crying. He then lashed me in the legs with kicks and knocked me to the floor. He kept kicking me but my son who was about four year old said "Stop kicking Mum." He ordered them to bed, further abused me verbally and physically, saying he would work the boot well into my ribs which he did. I pleaded with him to stop as I was expecting our third child.

He shouted at me: "Who is the father this time?" I think if my husband was seen by a doctor or a psychiatrist on that night he would be sedated or sent to a hospital.

My husband took a life on that night which he never had to account for. He made sure he locked all the doors so that nobody could come and help.

Before he went to bed he moved all the food out of the kitchen and locked me in the kitchen. He ordered me not to go upstairs to bed which I didn't. I had extreme pain and couldn't get a pain killer. I sat on a chair all night. In the morning when he got up he ordered me to go upstairs and not come down or meet anybody. I felt very weak and sore and knew then that I was going to lose the baby. My head was bursting with pain. I was a wreck. My eyes were sore from crying. Again I was wondering what that day would bring. It was sheer hell. I wished that the next time he went out he wouldn't come back.

I said to the children I'd need to go to a doctor. I endured another night of suffering. The next day I asked to go to the doctor as a I needed to. My husband would not allow this so I asked if I could go to the phone and speak to the doctor.

He followed me to the phone and stood by listening to the conversation so that I could not reveal how he treated me. The doctor came to the house and advised complete rest.

My husband warned me if I mentioned anything I would get more the next time. Eventually I had a miscarriage.

The doctor and midwife attended me at home. My husband said I was not going to hospital.

Nobody's Perfect

The Melrose Suspension Bridge spans the Niagara River in New York and links Canada and the United States.

They say that the bridge was built in the following way. First a kite was flown from across the river. Attached to the kite was a piece of string. Attached to the piece of string was a rope. And to the rope was attached a steel cable.

The steel cable was then used to get the rest of the bridge in place.

The story of the Melrose Bridge illustrates how great things often have humble beginnings. There's a modern trend which says: "I've no sin in my life so why do I need to ask forgiveness of anyone?"

I find it impossible to understand that view. I don't know of any life which hasn't faults, sins and hurt. I don't know of any life which doesn't need to seek forgiveness. Nobody's perfect.

These are some of the questions I keep asking myself.

1. Do I fit God into my life when it's convenient? What's the overriding thrust in my life? My own ambition? Career? Need for human respect? God's will?

2. What was the last decision I made which was guided solely by what God would want rather than what I would want?

3. When was the last time I gave up a permissible pleasure, knowing that I needed prayer more?

4. Do I build up or break down relationships with my family, my relatives, my fellow workers, my neighbours?

5. How much of my time and money and talent do I set aside out of compassion for the poor in the world, the suffering, the sick, the grieving? What has been my contribution to the furtherance of justice and the lessening of greed in the world?

6. Do I allow my moods at home or at work to control my environment? Are people afraid to approach me? Am I angry, bitter or resentful towards anyone?

7. Have I done anything to deal with the sin of anger in my life?

8. Have I forgiven everyone who has injured or offended me? Have I taken anyone's reputation by spreading even truthful stories,

and worse still, gossip or lies?

9. Have I an unhealthy thirst for power over others? At work? Or even fame and ambition?

10 What about spoiling the environment? What about spoiling my own mind? Obscene conversations? Sexism? Pornography? Violence?

11. Have I offended the Holy Spirit by trying to justify sins like abortion?

12. Have I helped spread sin by trying to be too worldly?

13. How important is truth in my life?

14. Have I abused my life, my family, or wasted my talents through the misuse of drugs, alcohol, food, money, time?

15. What about taking risks with the gift of faith? Like participating in a cult? Putting too much trust in fortune telling and palm reading and astrology? What superstitions are in my life? Is my religion too emotional, too superstitious?

I Saw A Bishop Cry

I saw a bishop cry that Tuesday.

It happened when Bishop John Kirby of Clonfert looked down at the 300 grieving priests, parishioners and family of Fr. Joe Walsh, seated in church, and raised his voice for the thousands standing numb and shocked outside in the rain. In front of him he saw the coffin of a young, quiet but immensely loved priest.

In his mind's eye, he saw the little white coffin of Liam Riney and beside it, Imelda Riney's, all three shot dead that week.

He remembered what everyone who saw Fr. Joe in his coffin before it was closed also remembered — a face which was changed by the pain of his last, violent hours.

He wrestled with the injustice of the fact that in death there was a frightened face on the man who brought peace to hundreds of others in their last hours on earth.

He saw the symbols of this priest's love for his people — his stole, his breviary, the colours of his beloved GAA club, all resting on the coffin.

On the altar before him were the gifts his people remembered Fr. Joe by — a hurley, a sliothar, a chalice, bread and wine and a china plate with the image of Our Lady of Clonfert on it.

He knew each symbol was equally religious and equally human. The bishop choked back a tear, took a deep breath and said exactly what we all wanted said.

"Fr. Joe Walsh was part of the hidden Ireland. He represents a huge number of good priests who give of their skills and talents for the benefit of a local community both in rural and urban settings.

"They are wayfarers themselves on the journey of life. They are pilgrim priests leading a pilgrim people."

The caring, local people regard this area on the borders of Clare and Galway as a corner of heaven.

Now, Bishop Kirby said, he and his people "lived in a cloud of fear, worry and confusion".

How could such an evil thing occur in such a heavenly place? It was an unspeakable tragedy for "a cluster of small communities, for the priests and the people... as well the families of Fr. Joe and

Imelda Riney and Liam."

They nodded and they sobbed. He put words on his people's desolation. "We ask: 'My God, my God, why have you forsaken me?' ... we acknowledge our feelings of abandonment and our sense of hurt and loss," he said.

His voice cracked and his brow furrowed. He was, like his people, heartbroken. And his great humanity was his best sermon.

A bishop cried at the death of his people and Christ was made visible in the midst of desolation.

In grief, honestly faced, there is hope. In small groups around this most beautiful of places, tired, numbed people and the whitened faces known best to those who are "cried out".

Their eyes were red and sad and questioning. A woman said to me: "Please write something next Sunday which will give us hope. For today I am not speaking to God."

She put her hand up to her mouth as if she had uttered a blasphemy. Then she said it again. Blasphemy or not, she was, rightly, going to have her say.

I took her hand. There are days when evil seems to have won. A lady with a round hat haloing a peace-filled face said she could cry no more but then told both of us:

"If you take your time, you'll see differently. Just because we can't see the reason, doesn't mean there is no plan. I just know good will come out of it."

A priest earlier said: "It would make you wonder. A young priest, a young mother, and a little boy."
And that's all he said. It was all there needed to be said. He had experienced the death of a Mr-Fixit-God.

A woman journeyed into a bottomless bag and showed me a photograph of Fr. Joe baptising her grandchild when he was a curate in Woodford.

"He was a lovely, approachable, emotional man. He laughed and he cried. The young ones loved him then. It was his first appointment. We called him the baby priest."

And you know that today that photo will be framed on the sideboard and Fr. Joe will never be forgotten.

"In a hundred years from now," the Bishop said, "people will remember that the curate in Eyrecourt died violently... in a hundred years from now I hope that the people will also remember that as a community we worked to develop further this spirit of caring and of healing."

He should not worry. These are good people who have not forgotten that there is such a thing as good grief.

It's uncomfortable for those who would rather not talk about death and who have suppressed grief. But these people will get back on their feet.

They will get over their guilt and their sadness. Their community will live again.

Then there was the aged wisdom of parish priest, Fr. Glynn. When he was in Ballinasloe, he welcomed Fr. Joe to the diocese to work as a young deacon.

That day he told him, "You're here to learn, but you're here to enjoy yourself too."

Kind words to a young man. Words never forgotten.

Later he welcomed him to Eyrecourt and earlier this year both had planned the funeral arrangements for Fr. Glynn. Instead, that Tuesday, the old man looked into the ground and said goodbye to his young friend. So unnatural. A community which confronts its grief like that will survive.

They need to be left alone to come to terms with the normal stages of grief — denial, anger, bargaining, depression and acceptance.

Life will never be the same again. It may be better or may be worse. But it will never be the same.

How could it when "a corner of heaven" lost a lovely innocent, little child, a devoted mother and a priest who believed enough in goodness to be fully human, fully alive?

No wonder the bishop cried.

Family

A family is a PLACE
to cry
and laugh
and vent frustrations
to ask for help
and tease
and yell
to be touched and hugged
and smiled at.

A family is PEOPLE
who care when you are sad
who love no matter what
who share your triumph
who don't expect you to be perfect
just growing with honesty in your own direction.

A family is a CIRCLE
where we learn to like ourselves
where we learn to make good decisions
where we learn to think before we do
where we learn integrity and
table manners and respect for other people
where we are special
where we share ideas
where we listen and are listened to
where we learn the rules of life
to prepare ourselves for the world

The world is a PLACE
where anything can happen.
If we grow up in a loving family
we are ready for the world.

Let's Crush Myths About Gay People

What does the Church say about gays? It's a simple question. If only the answer were as simple.

We need to clear the ground. It depends on which church.

A right wing fundamentalist church will snarl fire and brimstone and say it's evil, condemned for centuries and even in the Bible.

On the other hand you'll have some liberal churches claiming that gays and lesbians should be allowed to marry, be able to rear children and that there should be no distinction made between homosexuals and heterosexuals.

Somewhere in between you find the Catholic, Anglican and mainstream churches.

So at the risk of being misunderstood here are my random thoughts on how gays or lesbians are trying to find God in today's society.

Throughout my life I've met a huge number of gays and a significant number of lesbians. I've been changed, broadened and, I hope, made a better person by trying to walk with them in their struggle.

Twenty years ago I would have believed as most churches teach, that all lesbians and gays must be celibate for their entire lives if they are to do what God wants them.

After meeting many gays and lesbians in beautiful, caring, long-term couple relationships, I would find it much more difficult to believe that God gives the gifts of life-long abstinence to all lesbian and gay people.

At one time I would have accepted without question that homosexuality was an aberration or an illness. I always tried to treat them with kindness and as much understanding as possible. Looking back, I admit I probably was condescending in my attitude.

Now I know that there are many lesbian and gay people who are healthy and as normal sexually and psychologically, as the next person. Many of my myths haave been crushed.

Myths are the bane of all our lives!

• Myths like the presumption that gay men are effeminate and lesbians masculine. The facts are that 15 per cent of gay men fit the effeminate stereotype and less than 7 per cent of lesbians fit the masculine stereotype. Mostly, they are an invisible minority.

• The myths that gay men are promiscuous. It's difficult to get accurate information because, like the rest of us, they prefer to keep their sexual preferences and their sexual activity to themselves.

Gays and lesbians who are "out" seem to have many partners. But promiscuity could be part of the visibly gay sub-culture. There is no evidence to show that gays or lesbians in general are promiscuous.

• Myths about choice. A moral teacher I had as a student insisted that gays and lesbians had a choice. And at some point they made the choice to be gay or lesbian. I never really bought that myth but nevertheless many do.

The fact is that most don't choose to be lesbian or gay. They don't choose to have the feelings they have any more than heterosexual people do. Sexual orientation is not like that.

• Lastly, the myth that says that gays are over-sexed; that sex is all they think about and that they're attracted to everybody of the same sex. They're not.

When it comes to stating church teaching, it's more difficult. In general, Vatican statements cover five areas.

1. They state that genital activity among homosexuals is objectively wrong, insisting that lesbians and gays should be sexually abstinent.

Many moral theologians disagree. Theologians are divided on some issues. One group says that homosexual orientation is not normative. (I refuse to use the word "normal".) Other equally vocal theologians say that homosexual orientation is part of God's plan for creation and should be seen as positive, good and central to one's relationship with God and others.

But both groups of theologians will differ with the Catholic Church's assumption that genital activity is always objectively wrong. Many theologians will argue that, in certain circumstances, a gay or lesbian person in a commited relationship can be morally acceptable. At any rate, Vatican statements go further.

2.   They will agree that to be a homosexual is not wrong in itself.

3.   They insist that gays and lesbians should always be treated with great sensitivity and care. Homophobia is evil.

4.   Prejudice against lesbian and gay persons is a greater infringement of the Christian virtues than homosexual activity itself.

5.   All people, gays and lesbians most definitely included, have an intrinsic dignity which must be respected in law. If we say that sexual orientation is a good thing, why can't it be exercised? Why can't it be lived out in a loving, responsible way? Gays and lesbians are not trying to sanction promiscuous behaviour, rather they say that many same-sex loving relationships are good and fulfilling.

And I have to say that in practise the life and lifestyles of many mature, responsible couples bears that out. Somewhere down the line I hope the theologians and the official churches get together to make our churches more welcoming places for those who are different.

It is extremely difficult for homosexuals to grow up in a society which rejects them and in a community which says: "We think you're sinful."

The church never teaches that homosexuals are sinful but that's often a message that comes from church people. Could it be because so many heterosexual people have a difficulty in dealing with sexuality in an open, healthy manner themselves?

We must ensure that discrimination against homosexuals is never condoned. I believe that, in the hiring process, church institutions should not discriminate against a person mainly because he or she is homosexual. If that person is hired and subsequently discovered to be homosexual, then they shouldn't be fired, presuming there is no prefessional impropriety.

In sex education we need to get across, in the home and in the school, that homosexual as well as heterosexual feelings are normal, good and natural.

It's OK to feel sexual attraction. And it's normal for most people to have some homosexual feelings but it doesn't necessarily mean they will grow up to be lesbian or gay.

Finally, it's important for them to know that God loves and cares and many in the church do too. They may get a different impression from some church leaders and from church people they've met, but from some church leaders and from church people they've met, but there are many in the churches who care.

With the knowledge we now have, we need to ask pardon for the failure to accept and love our lesbian and gay children.

We must help lesbians and gays to grow up healthy and whole. That will help create a more balanced and loving environment for all of us, not just the gays.

Words of Wisdom

If you're going to have an exercise programme, start by exercising kindness. A word of encouragement during failure is worth more than a whole book of praise after a success.

Adam and Eve had many advantages but the principal one was that they escaped teething. (Mark Twain).

A government is the only vessel known to leak from the top.

Your last mistake is your best teacher.

You can give without loving, but you can't love without giving.

The Lord gave us two ends, one to sit on and the other to think with. Success depends on which one we use the more.

Think like a man of action, act like a man of thought.

The person who knows *how* has a job;
the person who knows *why* is the boss.

In youth we want to change the world.
In old age we want to change youth.

The young man knows the rules,
but the old man knows the exceptions.

Father Brian D'Arcy

Father Brian D'Arcy was born in Enniskillen, Co. Fermanagh in June 1945. He is one of a family of four, two boys and two girls. His father Hugh was a noted Gaelic footballer who played inter-county football for more than a decade.

He entered the Passionist Religious Congregation in 1962. He served for many years as parish priest at Mount Argus in Dublin, before returning to Enniskillen in 1989 as superior at St. Gabriel's Retreat, The Graan.

His career in journalism began in 1967 when he wrote regularly for various pop magazines at home and abroad. He was the first priest in Ireland to be admitted to the National Union of Journalists.

Brian D'Arcy is a well-known broadcaster and television personality. He has his own series of interviews on BBC Ulster and is "Pause For Thought" contributor on Terry Wogan's morning show on BBC Radio 2.

He has broadcast for 2 FM since its first day of broadcast and more recently has his own slot on RTE Radio 1 on "Both Sides Now".

He is a self-confessed "fanatical" sports enthusiast. Gaelic football is his favourite recreation but he's also well-known for his association with Shamrock Rovers and many of the international soccer players are his friends.

Among his more unusual pastimes is his voluntary role as chaplain to the entertainment industry. This brings him in close contact with the major personalities in pop music.

His favourite charity is the Helping Hand Fund, which helps the poor of Ireland, north and south. All proceeds from this book will go to the Helping Hand Fund.